# 365

Daily Insights from Historical Figures
Around the World

DAE LEE

Copyright © 2024 by Airplane Mode Publishing House

Second Edition Author: Dae Lee

All Rights Reserved.

No portion of this book may be reproduced in any form without written permission from the publisher or author, except as permitted by U.S. copyright law.

This publication is designed to provide accurate and authoritative information in regard to the subject matter covered. It is sold with the understanding that neither the author nor the publisher is engaged in rendering legal, investment, accounting or other professional services. While the publisher and author have used their best efforts in preparing this book, they make no representations or warranties with respect to the accuracy or completeness of the contents of this book and specifically disclaim any implied warranties of merchantability or fitness for a particular purpose. No warranty may be created or extended by sales representatives or written sales materials. The advice and strategies contained herein may not be suitable for your situation. You should consult with a professional when appropriate. Neither the publisher nor the author shall be liable for any loss of profit or any other commercial damages, including but not limited to special, incidental, consequential, personal, or other damages.

*For our Lou, whose spirit and joy remind us every day of the limitless potential and incredible strength found in every woman. May the stories in these pages inspire you as much as you inspire us.*

# CONTENTS

| | |
|---|---|
| January | 3 |
| February | 35 |
| March | 65 |
| April | 99 |
| May | 131 |
| June | 163 |
| July | 195 |
| August | 227 |
| September | 259 |
| October | 291 |
| November | 323 |
| December | 355 |
| Bonus | 387 |

# INTRODUCTION

Here we embark upon a journey through time and space, chronicling the lives of 365 women who have shaped the contours of our world. This book is a tapestry woven from the threads of women's experiences, triumphs, struggles, and indomitable spirits.

Each day, we encounter a new story, a new face, a new voice. From the ancient warrior queens who carved out empires, to the modern scientists unraveling the mysteries of the universe; from the artists whose palettes colored our perceptions, to the activists who fought tirelessly for equality and justice — their narratives are as diverse as humanity itself. These women, in their own unique ways, have defied conventions, surmounted insurmountable barriers, and left indelible marks on the annals of history.

Extending beyond to embrace a global perspective, this collection seeks to illuminate the oft-overlooked contributions of women. It is an homage to their resilience, a recognition of their contributions, and a celebration of their unyielding power to inspire.

To our dear daughter, born into a world rich with the legacies of these remarkable women, this book is dedicated to you. May their stories fill you with the courage to dream, the strength to persevere, and the wisdom to lead. May you find in these pages role models who speak to your heart and mentors who guide your steps. And above all, may you come to understand the vast expanse of what women can achieve.

For every reader who turns these pages, may you find a moment of connection, a spark of inspiration, a renewed sense of hope. This book is not merely a collection of biographies; it is a mosaic of possibilities, a reminder that every day holds the promise of inspiration, and that the stories of women are an integral part of the tapestry of our shared human experience.

In these stories, we find a reflection of our collective soul — a soul that perseveres, empowers, creates, and transforms. Let us delve into these lives with the reverence they deserve, and emerge enriched and inspired, ready to contribute our own verses to the enduring human epic.

Welcome to *365 Inspiring Women*. May these stories light your path, today and every day.

Dae Lee
@airplanemodepublishinghouse

365 INSPIRING WOMEN

# JANUARY

## 1 JANUARY

# Emily Dickinson

Pioneering American Poet

1830-1886, USA

Emily Dickinson, renowned for her profound and introspective poetry, stands as a towering figure in American literature. Known for her unique style and reclusive life, she penned nearly 1,800 poems. While only a few were published in her lifetime, her work gained immense popularity after her death. Despite her reclusive nature, Dickinson's exploration of themes like death, immortality, and nature resonates deeply with readers across generations.

Here's one of her beautiful poems:

> *There is no Frigate like a Book*
> *To take us Lands away*
> *Nor any Coursers like a Page*
> *Of prancing Poetry –*
> *This Traverse may the poorest take*
> *Without oppress of Toll –*
> *How frugal is the Chariot*
> *That bears the Human Soul*

**Did you know?** Emily rarely left her home and often communicated with friends through letters.

*"Forever is composed of nows."*

## 2 JANUARY

# Louisa May Alcott
Author of "Little Women"

1832-1888, USA

Louisa May Alcott, an American writer and pioneering feminist, achieved timeless fame with her novel 'Little Women. Growing up in a financially unstable home, she began working at a young age and used writing as an escape. "Little Women" mirrored her personal experiences, giving readers an insight into Alcott's own life. Apart from her literary achievements, she was an advocate for women's rights and abolition. Alcott's writing, often inspired by her own life experiences, blended rich character studies with insightful social commentary, particularly on the roles and rights of women.

*"I am not afraid of storms, for I am learning how to sail my ship."*

**Did you know?** Louisa also wrote under the pen name A. M. Barnard.

## 3 JANUARY

# Elizabeth Warren

U.S. Senator and Advocate for Financial Reforms

1949-Present, USA

Senator Elizabeth Warren, a prominent and influential figure in American politics, has dedicated her career to advocating for comprehensive financial reforms. As a law professor, she specialized in bankruptcy law. Later, she played a pivotal role in the creation of the Consumer Financial Protection Bureau. Her relentless pursuit of justice and transparency has made her a beloved figure among many.

*"Persistence is power."*

**Did you know?** Elizabeth was a schoolteacher before attending law school.

## 4 JANUARY

# Antonia Santos
Colombian Independence Heroine

1782-1819, Colombia

Antonia Santos, a pivotal figure in Colombia's struggle for independence from Spanish rule, exemplified courage and leadership. A brave leader, she used her home as a meeting place for rebels. Sadly, she was captured and executed by the Spanish, but her bravery and dedication are still remembered. Her role in organizing and supporting the rebellion, despite the risks, marks her as a symbol of resistance and national pride in Colombian history.

**Did you know?** Antonia is celebrated every year on July 28th in Colombia.

## 5 JANUARY

# Serena Williams
#### World Champion Tennis Player

1981-Present, USA

Serena Williams, with 23 Grand Slam titles, is often hailed as one of the greatest tennis players ever. Beyond her achievements on the court, she's an advocate for women's rights, especially in sports.

> *"I don't like to lose — at anything. Yet I've grown most not from victories, but setbacks."*

**Did you know?** Serena and her sister Venus have played against each other in nine Grand Slam singles finals.

## 6 JANUARY

# Maria Theresa

Empress of Austria

1717-1780, Austria

Maria Theresa ruled as the only female monarch of the Habsburg dominions. Taking the throne in challenging times, she implemented significant reforms in the realms of finance, education, and medicine.

**Did you know?** Maria Theresa had 16 children, one of whom was Marie Antoinette.

## 7 JANUARY

# Christina of Sweden

Queen Who Abdicated the Throne

1626-1689, Sweden

Queen Christina is best remembered for her decision to abdicate the Swedish throne. Highly educated, she valued art and culture, inviting many scholars to her court. Her reign, though brief, was marked by a passionate patronage of arts and philosophy, creating a vibrant cultural legacy in Sweden.

**Did you know?** Christina was one of the few women buried in the Vatican grotto.

## 8 JANUARY

# Irena Sendler
### Savior of Warsaw's Jews

1910-2008, Poland

During World War II, Irena Sendler bravely saved over 2,500 Jewish children by smuggling them out of the Warsaw Ghetto. Despite being captured and tortured, she never revealed any names.

*"Every child saved with my help is the justification of my existence on this Earth."*

**Did you know?** Irena kept records of all the children's real names, hoping to reunite them with their families after the war.

## 9 JANUARY

# Marsha P. Johnson

LGBTQ+ Activist

1945-1992, USA

Marsha P. Johnson, a prominent figure in the Stonewall Uprising, was an outspoken advocate for gay rights during a time of widespread discrimination. She co-founded the Gay Liberation Front and the Street Transvestite Action Revolutionaries.

*"No pride for some of us without liberation for all of us."*

**Did you know?** Marsha's "P" stood for "Pay It No Mind," which was her response to those who questioned her gender.

## 10 JANUARY

# Isabella I of Castile
Queen of the Spanish Golden Age

1451-1504, Spain

Isabella I, alongside King Ferdinand, united Spain and set the stage for its Golden Age. A patron of Christopher Columbus, her rule expanded Spain's territories, and she implemented significant internal reforms.

**Did you know?** Isabella was proclaimed queen at a town called Segovia.

## 11 JANUARY

# Cleopatra

Last Pharaoh of Ancient Egypt

69-30 BCE, Egypt

Cleopatra VII, often simply called Cleopatra, was the last active ruler of the Ptolemaic Kingdom of Egypt. As a diplomat, naval commander, linguist, and medical author, Cleopatra was one of the most influential women of her time. Her romantic liaisons and military alliances with Roman leaders Julius Caesar and Mark Antony have been immortalized in historical and dramatic writings.

*"I will not be triumphed over."*

**Did you know?** Cleopatra was not Egyptian; she was of Macedonian Greek origin and was the first of her family to learn the Egyptian language.

## 12 JANUARY

# Catherine the Great
Empress of Russia

1729-1796, Russia

Born as Princess Sophie of Anhalt-Zerbst, Catherine became the longest-ruling female leader of Russia. Her reign was marked by vast territorial expansion, modernization, and a cultural renaissance, turning Russia into one of the great powers of Europe.

*"I beg you take courage; the brave soul can mend even disaster."*

**Did you know?** Catherine was an avid art collector; her collection laid the foundation for the Hermitage Museum in St. Petersburg.

## 13 JANUARY

# Sophie Scholl

Anti-Nazi Activist

1921-1943, Germany

Sophie Scholl, a young university student, was a key member of the White Rose non-violent resistance group against the Nazis. Her courage in distributing anti-Nazi leaflets, knowing the risks, became a beacon of defiance against oppressive regimes.

*"Stand up for what you believe in even if you are standing alone."*

**Did you know?** Sophie and her brother were arrested after a leaflet drop at the University of Munich and were executed just a few days later.

## 14 JANUARY

# Caresse Crosby
Inventor of the Modern Bra

1891-1970, USA

Caresse Crosby, born Mary Phelps Jacob, revolutionized women's fashion by inventing the first modern bra. Tired of the restrictive corsets of her time, she crafted a garment made of two handkerchiefs and ribbon. Beyond her invention, she was a patron of the arts and a key figure in the Lost Generation literary scene. Her invention, liberating women from the confines of corsets, was a significant step forward in the women's liberation movement and reflected her broader contributions to art and culture.

*"Inspiration is the thread of our dreams, creation the path of our reality."*

**Did you know?** Caresse and her husband founded the Black Sun Press, publishing works of many famous authors including Ernest Hemingway.

## 15 JANUARY

# Susan La Flesche Picotte

First Native American Physician

1865-1915, USA

Susan, an Omaha Native American, became the first Native American woman to earn a medical degree in the U.S. Overcoming racial and gender biases, she tirelessly served her community, advocating for better health and living conditions for the Omaha people. Her extraordinary dedication to medicine and her people's welfare, overcoming both racial and gender barriers, has made her a role model for aspiring physicians and advocates for indigenous rights.

*"Everything I am today, I owe to my faith and my work in medicine."*

**Did you know?** Susan often worked 20-hour days and covered vast territories to ensure her patients got the care they needed.

## 16 JANUARY

# Ching Shih

Most Powerful Pirate in History

1775-1844, China

Ching Shih, formerly a prostitute, became one of the most powerful pirates in history. Commanding the infamous Red Flag Fleet, she challenged the Qing Dynasty, British, and Portuguese empires with her might.

**Did you know?** At the height of her power, Ching Shih's command included 300 junks and 20,000-40,000 pirates.

## 19 JANUARY

# Dorothy Parker

Acclaimed American Writer and Wit

1893-1967, USA

Dorothy Parker was known for her sharp wit, biting satire, and short stories. A founding member of the Algonquin Round Table, an esteemed group of New York City writers, she became a notable figure in 20th-century literature.

*"Wit has truth in it; wisecracking is simply calisthenics with words."*

**Did you know?** Dorothy wrote for *Vogue* and *Vanity Fair* before getting involved in Hollywood screenwriting.

## 20 JANUARY

# Jocelyn Bell Burnell

Discoverer of Radio Pulsars

1943-Present, UK

Jocelyn Bell Burnell, an astrophysicist, co-discovered the first radio pulsars in 1967. This groundbreaking discovery was awarded a Nobel Prize, though Jocelyn did not receive the honor. However, she gracefully continued her significant contributions to science.

*"We have to be the change we want. It's up to us."*

**Did you know?** In 2018, Jocelyn was awarded the Special Breakthrough of the Year award and donated her entire winnings to help female, minority, and refugee students become physics researchers.

## 21 JANUARY

# Lucille Ball
Queen of Comedy

1911-1989, USA

Lucille Ball, with her unmistakable fiery red hair, became one of America's beloved television stars. Her iconic show "I Love Lucy" showcased her comedic genius and revolutionized television production. Along with her husband Desi Arnaz, Ball founded Desilu Productions, producing numerous popular television series.

*"I'm not funny. What I am is brave."*

**Did you know?** Lucille was the first woman to run a major television studio, Desilu Productions.

## 22 JANUARY

# Zitkala-Sa

Native American Writer and Activist

1876-1938, USA

Born on the Yankton Sioux reservation, Zitkala-Sa, also known as Gertrude Simmons Bonnin, became an influential writer, musician, and activist. Her works shed light on Native American experiences, blending her heritage with Western musical and literary forms.

*"I was neither a wee girl nor a tall one; neither a wild Indian nor a tame one."*

**Did you know?** Zitkala-Sa co-composed the first Native American opera, "The Sun Dance Opera."

## 23 JANUARY

# Gloria Steinem

Feminist Icon and Journalist

1934-Present, USA

Gloria Steinem is a groundbreaking journalist and social-political activist recognized as a leader of the American feminist movement. Co-founding *Ms.* magazine, she used her platform to advocate for women's rights and equality, challenging societal norms and policies.

> *"The truth will set you free, but first it will piss you off."*

**Did you know?** Gloria went undercover as a Playboy Bunny in 1963 to expose the working conditions at the Playboy Club.

## 24 JANUARY

# Dorothy Day

Advocate for the Poor and Peace

1897-1980, USA

Dorothy Day co-founded the Catholic Worker Movement, dedicated to aiding the poor and fighting for social justice. Through *The Catholic Worker* newspaper, she voiced issues of inequality, pacifism, and the need for social reform in the midst of the Great Depression.

*"People say, 'What is the sense of our small effort?' They cannot see that we must lay one brick at a time, take one step at a time."*

**Did you know?** Dorothy was arrested multiple times during her life for her peace activism and protests.

## 25 JANUARY

# Alaa Salah

Sudanese Revolution Symbol

1996-Present, Sudan

Alaa Salah emerged as a symbol of Sudan's anti-government protests in 2019. An image of her, clad in white and standing atop a car leading chants, went viral, capturing the spirit of a nation seeking change. She represents the critical role of women in the revolution and their demands for a better future.

*"The bullet doesn't kill. What kills is the silence of people."*

**Did you know?** Alaa is a student of architectural engineering and was only 22 when she became an icon of the Sudanese protests.

## 26 JANUARY
# Funmilayo Ransome-Kuti
Nigerian Women's Rights Activist

1900-1978, Nigeria

Funmilayo Ransome-Kuti, a passionate educator and activist, played a pivotal role in granting Nigerian women the right to vote. She was also the first woman to drive a car in Nigeria and was instrumental in challenging and changing British colonial policies.

*"I have never been 'sensible'."*

**Did you know?** Her son, Fela Kuti, is internationally renowned for pioneering the Afrobeat music genre.

## 27 JANUARY

# Shirin Neshat
Iranian Visual Artist

1957-Present, Iran/USA

Shirin Neshat's art poignantly addresses issues of exile, identity, and feminism. Her photographs and video installations offer deep insights into the lives of Muslim women and challenge Western preconceptions about the role of women in Islamic societies.

*"Art is our weapon. Culture is a form of resistance."*

**Did you know?** Shirin won the Silver Lion for Best Director at the 66th Venice Film Festival for her directorial debut, "Women Without Men."

## 28 JANUARY

# Shirley Chisholm

First Black Woman Elected to U.S. Congress

1924-2005, USA

Shirley Chisholm shattered multiple glass ceilings in her lifetime. In 1968, she became the first black woman elected to the U.S. Congress, representing New York's 12th Congressional District. In 1972, she was the first black woman from a major party to run for the U.S. presidency.

*"If they don't give you a seat at the table, bring a folding chair."*

**Did you know?** Shirley survived three assassination attempts during her presidential campaign.

## 29 JANUARY

# Dolores Huerta

Labor Leader and Civil Rights Activist

1930-Present, USA

Dolores Huerta, alongside Cesar Chavez, co-founded the United Farm Workers (UFW). Her tireless advocacy has resulted in improvements for union workers' rights, immigrants, and women.

> *"Every moment is an organizing opportunity, every person a potential activist, every minute a chance to change the world."*

**Did you know?** Dolores coined the famous phrase, "¡Sí, se puede!" (Yes, we can!).

## 30 JANUARY

# Empress Irene of the Byzantine Empire

Restorer of Icons

c. 752-803, Byzantine Empire

Irene ruled as Empress Regent for her son and later as sole Empress. She's best known for ending the Iconoclast Controversy by restoring the veneration of icons in the Eastern Orthodox Church.

**Did you know?** Empress Irene convened the Second Council of Nicaea in 787, which reversed the ban on religious icons.

## 31 JANUARY

# Gilda Radner

Comedic Genius and Original SNL Cast Member

1946-1989, USA

Gilda Radner, with her unique comedic style and memorable characters, became one of the original cast members of Saturday Night Live (SNL). Through her sketches, she brought joy and laughter to millions.

> *"I wanted a perfect ending. Now I've learned, the hard way, that some poems don't rhyme, and some stories don't have a clear beginning, middle, and end."*

**Did you know?** Gilda was posthumously awarded an Emmy for her one-woman Broadway show, "Gilda Live."

365 INSPIRING WOMEN

# FEBRUARY

## 1 FEBRUARY

# Queen Sheba

### Legendary Ruler of Sheba

c. 10th century BCE, Kingdom of Sheba

The captivating Queen Sheba is renowned for her journey across the desert to meet King Solomon of Israel. Their encounter is wrapped in mystery, romance, and diplomacy. Sheba's story, which appears in biblical, Islamic, and Ethiopian texts, illustrates a woman of wit, curiosity, and intelligence, leaving a lasting impact on multiple cultures.

*"The half was not told me; you exceed in wisdom and prosperity the report that I heard." — Words attributed to Queen Sheba upon meeting King Solomon, 1 Kings 10:7*

**Did you know?** Queen Sheba is believed to have introduced the spice trade to the Israelites.

## 2 FEBRUARY

# Queen Nzinga of Ndongo and Matamba

Fearless African Monarch

1583-1663, Angola

Queen Nzinga was a masterful diplomat, military strategist, and visionary leader. Facing threats from Portuguese slave traders, she adeptly formed alliances and resisted colonial domination to ensure her people's freedom.

> *"I am a woman, but I can assure you that I am as brave as any man."*

**Did you know?** Queen Nzinga often dressed in male warrior attire and led her troops into battle.

## 3 FEBRUARY

# Yoko Ono

Artist, Singer, and Peace Activist

1933-Present, Japan/USA

Yoko Ono, often polarizing yet undeniably influential, has constantly evolved as an artist. Her avant-garde art and music challenge conventional norms. Beyond her marriage to John Lennon, Ono's peace activism and innovative art installations have made her a standout figure in cultural history.

*"A dream you dream alone is only a dream. A dream you dream together is reality."*

**Did you know?** Yoko Ono's "Wish Trees" art installations invite people to tie wishes to tree branches.

## 4 FEBRUARY

# Tomoe Gozen
### Famed Female Samurai

c. 1157-1247, Japan

Tomoe Gozen is one of the few recognized female samurai warriors in Japanese history. Skilled in archery and sword fighting, she fought in numerous battles, displaying unparalleled bravery and earning a place in Japan's legendary warrior tales.

*"She was a fearless rider whom neither the fiercest horse nor the roughest ground could dismay."* — The Tale of the Heike

**Did you know?** Tomoe Gozen was known to have taken down several prominent samurai warriors in battle.

## 5 FEBRUARY

# Mary Seacole
Pioneer Nurse and Healer

1805-1881, Jamaica

Born in Jamaica and of mixed-race descent, Mary Seacole combined traditional Caribbean and African healing methods with Western medicine to treat wounded soldiers during the Crimean War. She funded her own trip to the war zone after being rejected by British war authorities and set up the "British Hotel" to care for soldiers.

> *"I have a few shades of deeper brown upon my skin which shows me related to those poor mortals you once held enslaved."*

**Did you know?** Mary Seacole self-financed her journey to the Crimean War using her savings.

## 6 FEBRUARY
# Aung San Suu Kyi
Advocate for Democracy in Myanmar

1945-Present, Myanmar

Aung San Suu Kyi spent nearly 15 years under house arrest for her peaceful resistance against Myanmar's military regime. Awarded the Nobel Peace Prize in 1991, she remains a symbol for non-violent struggle for democracy and human rights. However, her reputation was later clouded by controversies surrounding Myanmar's treatment of the Rohingya minority.

*"It is not power that corrupts but fear. Fear of losing power corrupts those who wield it."*

**Did you know?** Aung San Suu Kyi is the daughter of General Aung San, considered the father of modern-day Myanmar.

## 7 FEBRUARY

# Frances Perkins

First Female U.S. Cabinet Member

1880-1965, USA

Frances Perkins served as the U.S. Secretary of Labor from 1933 to 1945, the first woman to hold a cabinet position in the U.S. government. She played a pivotal role in implementing the New Deal policies during the Great Depression, including the establishment of Social Security.

*"Being a woman has only bothered me in climbing trees."*

**Did you know?** Frances witnessed the tragic Triangle Shirtwaist Factory fire in 1911, which deeply influenced her commitment to workers' rights.

## 8 FEBRUARY

# Huda Sha'arawi

Egyptian Feminist and Activist

1879-1947, Egypt

Huda Sha'arawi was a pioneering feminist in the Arab world. She founded Egypt's first feminist organization and women's journal. A staunch advocate for women's rights, her act of removing her veil publicly symbolized a call for greater freedom for Egyptian women.

*"Men have singled out women of outstanding merit and put them on a pedestal to avoid recognizing the capabilities of all women."*

**Did you know?** Huda played a significant role in initiating the Egyptian Feminist Union in 1923.

## 9 FEBRUARY

# Jane Goodall

World-renowned Primatologist and Conservationist

1934-Present, England/Tanzania

Dr. Jane Goodall transformed the world's understanding of primates through her groundbreaking research on wild chimpanzees in Tanzania. Her discoveries about chimp behavior emphasized the close relationship between humans and animals.

> *"What you do makes a difference, and you have to decide what kind of difference you want to make."*

**Did you know?** Jane Goodall began her work without formal training, only a notebook and binoculars.

## 10 FEBRUARY
# Barbara McClintock
Nobel Prize-winning Geneticist

1902-1992, USA

Barbara McClintock's groundbreaking work in genetics on maize plants led to the discovery of "jumping genes," altering our understanding of genetic inheritance. Her innovative research earned her the Nobel Prize in Physiology or Medicine in 1983.

*"If you know you are on the right track, if you have this inner knowledge, then nobody can turn you off.. no matter what they say."*

**Did you know?** For years, the scientific community overlooked Barbara's findings, but her persistence eventually changed the world of genetics.

## 11 FEBRUARY

# Queen Yaa Asantewaa
Fierce Leader of the Ashanti Uprising

1840-1921, Ghana

Queen Yaa Asantewaa led the Ashanti resistance against British colonial rule. As a warrior queen, she stood as a symbol of female empowerment in a traditionally male-dominated society.

*"If you, the men of Ashanti, will not go forward, then we will. We, the women, will."*

**Did you know?** Her leadership in the War of the Golden Stool was the last major war led by an African woman against European colonizers.

## 12 FEBRUARY

# Amelia Bloomer

American Women's Rights Advocate

1818-1894, USA

Amelia Bloomer championed women's rights and is best remembered for popularizing the "bloomer," a type of women's clothing. As the editor of *The Lily*, she promoted suffrage and temperance movements.

*"When you find a burden in belief or apparel, cast it off."*

**Did you know?** *The Lily* was the first newspaper by and for women.

## 13 FEBRUARY

# Mae Jemison

First Black Woman in Space

1956-Present, USA

Dr. Mae Jemison, an engineer, physician, and former NASA astronaut, became the first black woman to travel in space aboard the Space Shuttle Endeavour. Beyond her space travel, she's an advocate for science education and a dancer.

> *"Never be limited by other people's limited imaginations."*

**Did you know?** Mae took a photo of the Alvin Ailey American Dance Theater to space, blending her love for science and dance.

## 14 FEBRUARY

# Shirley Jackson

Acclaimed Horror and Mystery Writer

1916-1965, USA

Shirley Jackson's writings have captivated readers with their eerie narratives and profound reflections on the human psyche. Her story, *The Lottery*, remains a significant commentary on society's blind adherence to tradition.

*"I delight in what I fear."*

**Did you know?** Shirley often explored the theme of alienation and isolation in suburban settings.

## 15 FEBRUARY

# Amal Clooney
Renowned Human Rights Lawyer

1978-Present, Lebanon/UK

Amal Clooney, an internationally recognized human rights lawyer, has represented a variety of clients, from political prisoners to ousted heads of state. Her dedication to justice and fairness has cemented her reputation in the legal world.

*"The worst thing that we can do as women is not stand up for each other."*

**Did you know?** Amal has taught at several universities, including Columbia Law School.

## 16 FEBRUARY

# Trưng Trắc

Vietnamese Warrior and Heroine

1st Century AD, Vietnam

Trưng Trắc, along with her sister Trưng Nhị, led an uprising against the Chinese Han Dynasty rulers to gain independence for Vietnam. For three years, she ruled as the Queen Regent, establishing herself as a symbol of resistance and courage.

*"When our nation is in need, how can a woman sit idle?"*

**Did you know?** The annual Hát Trưng festival in Vietnam commemorates the sisters' revolt against the Han Dynasty.

## 17 FEBRUARY

# Billie Holiday

Iconic Jazz and Blues Singer

1915-1959, USA

Billie Holiday's unique voice and raw emotional delivery made her one of the greatest jazz vocalists of all time. Despite facing many personal and societal challenges, including racism, her legacy endures in classics like "Strange Fruit."

*"I sing like I feel."*

**Did you know?** Billie's poignant song "Strange Fruit" was a protest against racial lynchings.

## 18 FEBRUARY

# Vera Rubin

Astronomer and Pioneer of Dark Matter

1928-2016, USA

Vera Rubin's observations of galaxies led to a groundbreaking discovery: the presence of dark matter. She challenged established notions in astronomy and paved the way for future studies on the universe's unseen components.

*"Science progresses best when observations force us to alter our preconceptions."*

**Did you know?** Vera often faced gender discrimination but persisted, becoming the only woman in her graduate class at Princeton.

## 19 FEBRUARY

# Fadumo Dayib

Presidential Candidate and Public Health Advocate

1972-Present, Finland/Somalia

Born a refugee in Kenya and later relocating to Finland, Fadumo Dayib returned to Somalia as an adult, aiming to bring change. Despite receiving death threats, she ran for president in Somalia in 2016, fighting for a more inclusive government.

*"I owe it to the 11-year-old girl I was... to go back and create an environment where young girls can aspire to become the leaders of tomorrow."*

**Did you know?** Fadumo has a Master's in Public Administration from Harvard University.

## 20 FEBRUARY

# Bessie Coleman

First African-American and Native American Woman Pilot

1892-1926, USA

Breaking both gender and racial barriers, Bessie Coleman became a licensed pilot when aviation schools in the U.S. denied her entry. Traveling to France to train, she returned as a celebrated daredevil and stunt flyer.

*"The air is the only place free from prejudices."*

**Did you know?** Bessie performed aerial tricks, parachuted, and gave lectures to inspire others.

## 21 FEBRUARY

# Mary Kom

Six-time World Amateur Boxing Champion

1982-Present, India

Mary Kom's fierce determination in the boxing ring has made her an icon in India and around the world. Balancing her roles as a mother and athlete, she has faced and triumphed over numerous challenges in her career.

> *"Don't let anyone tell you you're weak because you're a woman."*

**Did you know?** Mary Kom is nicknamed "Magnificent Mary" for her incredible boxing feats.

## 22 FEBRUARY

# Bess Truman

First Lady and Unsung Backbone of Truman Presidency

1885-1982, USA

Bess Truman, born Elizabeth Virginia Wallace, was a significant figure during one of the most pivotal eras in American history. Serving as First Lady from 1945 to 1953, during her husband Harry S. Truman's presidency, Bess was known for her strong-willed nature and unwavering support for her family.

Though she often preferred to stay out of the public eye, Bess was an essential advisor and confidante to President Truman. Her insights were highly valued by her husband, especially in matters beyond the domestic sphere. She was quietly influential, contributing to decision-making processes and offering counsel during critical times in her husband's presidency.

*"A woman's place in public is to sit beside her husband, be silent, and be sure her hat is on straight."*

**Did you know?** Bess Truman is one of the longest-lived First Ladies in American history, living to the age of 97. Her long life allowed her to experience and be part of a remarkable span of American history, from the era of horse-drawn carriages to the dawn of the space age.

## 23 FEBRUARY

# Maria Martinez

Master Potter and Native American Art Revitalizer

1887-1980, San Ildefonso Pueblo, New Mexico

Known for her exquisite black-on-black pottery, Maria Martinez revived and innovated traditional Pueblo pottery techniques. Her art has been celebrated globally, showcasing the rich cultural heritage of the Pueblo people.

> *"When we say that pottery is made in the old way, it means that only native clays and materials are used, and everything is done by hand."*

**Did you know?** Maria's pottery techniques became a family tradition, passed down through generations.

## 24 FEBRUARY
# Sister Rosetta Tharpe
Gospel's First Superstar and Godmother of Rock and Roll

1915-1973, USA

Blending gospel with rhythm, blues, and jazz, Sister Rosetta Tharpe became one of the first great recording stars of gospel music. Her innovative style influenced many of rock and roll's founding figures.

*"There's something inside of me, something I've never sold."*

**Did you know?** Sister Rosetta played an electric guitar, challenging norms for both her gender and her musical genre.

## 25 FEBRUARY

# Dolly Parton

**Legendary Country Music Singer and Philanthropist**

1946-Present, USA

From humble beginnings in a one-room cabin in Tennessee, Dolly Parton has become an international icon in country music. With her distinctive voice, she's penned classics like "Jolene." Beyond music, Dolly's philanthropy has touched millions.

*"Find out who you are and do it on purpose."*

**Did you know?** Dolly's Imagination Library program has donated over 100 million books to children.

## 26 FEBRUARY

# Julia de Burgos
### Celebrated Puerto Rican Poet

1914-1953, Puerto Rico

Through her profound poetry, Julia de Burgos tackled complex themes such as love, feminism, and national identity. Her works remain influential, resonating with the struggles and aspirations of Puerto Ricans.

*"I am life, strength, woman."*

**Did you know?** Julia was also an advocate for Puerto Rican independence.

## 27 FEBRUARY

# Queen Margaret I of Denmark

Unifier of Scandinavia

1353-1412, Denmark

Margaret I's diplomatic and strategic acumen paved the way for the Kalmar Union, uniting Denmark, Norway, and Sweden under one monarch. Her rule brought relative peace and prosperity to the region.

**Did you know?** Margaret effectively became the leader of Denmark at the age of 10, following her father's death.

## 28 FEBRUARY

# Bessie Smith

Empress of the Blues

1894-1937, USA

One of the most popular singers of the 1920s and 1930s, Bessie Smith's powerful voice and soulful renditions made her a leading figure in the blues genre. Despite facing racial prejudices, she dominated the music industry.

> *"I ain't good-looking, but I'm somebody's angel child."*

**Did you know?** Bessie was the highest-paid black entertainer of her time.

## 29 FEBRUARY

# Jacqueline Kennedy Onassis
Iconic First Lady and Cultural Preservationist

1929-1994, USA

Jacqueline Kennedy Onassis remains one of the most iconic First Ladies in U.S. history. Beyond her elegance, she was passionate about cultural preservation, ensuring that historic White House interiors were authentically restored.

> *"Once you can express yourself, you can tell the world what you want from it."*

**Did you know?** Jacqueline was also an accomplished book editor in her later life.

365 INSPIRING WOMEN

# MARCH

## 1 MARCH

# Michelle Obama

Former First Lady and Advocate for Healthy Living

1964-Present, USA

Growing up in the South Side of Chicago, Michelle Obama excelled academically, leading her to Princeton and then Harvard Law. As First Lady, she championed healthy eating, military families, and education. Her memoir, "Becoming," offers a deeply personal account of her life.

*"Success isn't about how much money you make; it's about the difference you make in people's lives."*

**Did you know?** Michelle skipped the second grade because of her advanced reading level.

## 2 MARCH

# Ynes Mexia

Pioneering Botanist and Explorer

1870-1938, USA/Mexico

Starting her botany career at 55, Ynes Mexia went on extraordinary expeditions, collecting more than 150,000 specimens. Her work significantly contributed to the understanding of plant species in the Americas.

*"The fascination of any search after truth lies not in the attainment... but in the pursuit."*

**Did you know?** Ynes survived earthquakes, treacherous terrains, and even a plane crash during her expeditions.

## 3 MARCH

# Rigoberta Menchú

Indigenous Rights Activist and Nobel Peace Prize Winner

1959-Present, Guatemala

Facing persecution and violence in her early life due to her indigenous heritage, Rigoberta Menchú became a vocal advocate for the rights of indigenous peoples in Central America, earning her the Nobel Peace Prize in 1992.

*"We are not myths of the past, ruins in the jungle, or zoos. We are people and we want to be respected, not to be victims of intolerance and racism."*

**Did you know?** Menchú ran for the presidency of Guatemala in 2007 and 2011.

## 4 MARCH

# Queen Tomyris
### Fierce Leader of the Massagetae

6th Century BCE, Central Asia

After the Persians, under Cyrus the Great, captured her son, Tomyris led her troops into a victorious battle against one of the mightiest empires, ensuring the Massagetae remained independent and feared.

*"I warned you that I would quench your thirst for blood, and so I shall."*

**Did you know?** Tomyris is often depicted in art, symbolizing female courage and power.

## 5 MARCH

# Dorothy Crowfoot Hodgkin

Pioneering X-ray Crystallographer

1910-1994, United Kingdom

Dorothy's dedication to understanding the structures of important biochemical substances using X-ray crystallography led to the discovery of the structures of penicillin, vitamin B12, and insulin. She was awarded the Nobel Prize in Chemistry in 1964.

*"In science, I soon learned, you did things because you enjoyed them."*

**Did you know?** Dorothy continued her research even during the bombings of World War II.

## 6 MARCH

# Gorgo, Queen of Sparta
### Wise Spartan Queen

5th Century BCE, Sparta

As the wife of King Leonidas I, Gorgo was known not only for her beauty but also her wisdom and political acumen. She played a crucial role in the political landscape of ancient Sparta and was deeply respected.

**Did you know?** Gorgo once advised her father on a diplomatic matter, showcasing her early involvement in politics.

## 7 MARCH

# Aimee Semple McPherson

Evangelist and Media Pioneer

1890-1944, USA

Aimee was one of the most glamorous women in the US during the 1920s and 1930s. She was known for her theatrical church services and was a pioneer in using radio to reach a larger audience for her evangelical messages.

> *"I have sipped enough nectar from the roses of Shiraz, and it's time to go."*

**Did you know?** Aimee once disappeared, causing a nationwide sensation, only to reappear later claiming she had been kidnapped.

## 8 MARCH

# Mitsuye Endo
Civil Rights Advocate

1920-2006, USA

During WWII, when Japanese-Americans were forcibly interned, Mitsuye Endo resisted. Her legal challenge reached the Supreme Court, resulting in the release of thousands from the internment camps.

**Did you know?** The Endo case played a pivotal role in ending the internment of Japanese-Americans.

## 9 MARCH

# Dorothea Dix
Advocate for the Mentally Ill

1802-1887, USA

Observing the dire conditions of mental asylums, Dorothea Dix campaigned rigorously for humane treatment. Her efforts led to the establishment of 32 institutions dedicated to the mentally ill across the US.

*"I proceed, gentlemen, briefly to call your attention to the present state of insane persons confined within this Commonwealth."*

**Did you know?** Dix volunteered as the Superintendent of Army Nurses during the Civil War.

## 10 MARCH
# Manuela Sáenz
Revolutionary Heroine of South America

1797-1856, Ecuador/Peru

A staunch supporter of Simón Bolívar and a revolutionary in her own right, Manuela Sáenz earned the title "Libertadora del Libertador" (Liberator of the Liberator) for saving Bolívar from an assassination attempt.

*"I offer you my life, my love, and my service until death."*

**Did you know?** Manuela was posthumously promoted to the rank of General by the Ecuadorian government in 2007.

## 11 MARCH

# Aretha Franklin
The Queen of Soul

1942-2018, USA

From singing in her father's church to becoming the "Queen of Soul," Aretha Franklin's unparalleled vocal prowess earned her international acclaim. Her iconic hits, such as "Respect" and "Chain of Fools," were not just musically influential but also anthems of civil rights and feminism.

*"Music does a lot of things for a lot of people. It's transporting, for sure. It can take you right back, years back, to the very moment certain things happened in your life."*

**Did you know?** Aretha Franklin was the first woman to be inducted into the Rock and Roll Hall of Fame in 1987.

## 12 MARCH

# Audre Lorde
Writer and Civil Rights Activist

1934-1992, USA

Audre Lorde's powerful prose and poetry tackled issues of race, gender, and sexuality. A self-described "black, lesbian, mother, warrior, poet," Lorde's writings remain influential, challenging societal norms and advocating for equality.

*"Your silence will not protect you."*

**Did you know?** Lorde co-founded Kitchen Table: Women of Color Press, the first U.S. publisher for women of color.

## 13 MARCH

# Rosalind Franklin

Pioneer in DNA Research

1920-1958, UK

Although often overlooked in her time, Rosalind Franklin's expertise in X-ray diffraction was pivotal in discovering the double helix structure of DNA. Her photograph, "Photo 51," inspired Watson and Crick's model of DNA.

*"Science and everyday life cannot and should not be separated."*

**Did you know?** Rosalind also conducted important research on viruses, laying the groundwork for structural virology.

## 14 MARCH

# Anne Frank

Diarist During the Holocaust

1929-1945, the Netherlands

In her diary, Anne Frank documented her life in hiding during WWII due to Nazi persecution. Though she tragically died in a concentration camp, her writings live on, offering a personal glimpse into the effects of prejudice and hatred.

*"Despite everything, I believe that people are really good at heart."*

**Did you know?** Anne's diary has been translated into over 70 languages and has sold millions of copies worldwide.

## 15 MARCH

# Ida Tarbell

Investigative Journalist and Muckraker

1857-1944, USA

Ida Tarbell, a leading journalist in the Progressive Era, is best remembered for her pioneering investigative reporting on the Standard Oil Company, which led to the corporation's breakup. She highlighted the dangers of unchecked corporate power.

> *"The quest of the truth had been born in me - the most tragic and incomplete, as well as the most essential, of man's quests."*

**Did you know?** Tarbell's investigative journalism techniques set standards for future journalists.

## 16 MARCH

# Beyoncé Knowles-Carter
Global Music Icon and Philanthropist

1981-Present, USA

Beyoncé Giselle Knowles-Carter has not only become a defining figure in modern music but also a powerful symbol of female empowerment and cultural influence. Rising to fame in the late 1990s as the lead singer of Destiny's Child, one of the world's best-selling girl groups, Beyoncé embarked on a solo career that propelled her to global stardom. Her music, known for its captivating blend of R&B, pop, and hip hop, is not just entertainment but a vehicle for social commentary and advocacy. Beyoncé's lyrics often reflect themes of love, relationships, and female strength, resonating deeply with a wide audience.

As a philanthropist, Beyoncé has used her influence to champion various causes. She co-founded the Survivor Foundation to provide transitional housing for victims of Hurricane Katrina and has been actively involved in campaigns for education, women's rights, and Black Lives Matter. Her charitable work extends to global humanitarian efforts, supporting initiatives like the Global Citizen Festival and Chime for Change.

*"Power is not given to you. You have to take it."*

**Did you know?** Beyoncé was the first black woman to headline the Coachella music festival in 2018.

## 17 MARCH

# Barbara Jordan

Trailblazing Politician and Civil Rights Leader

1936-1996, USA

Barbara Jordan shattered racial and gender barriers, becoming the first Southern African-American woman elected to the U.S. House of Representatives. Her eloquence and integrity, especially during the Nixon impeachment, solidified her legacy.

*"What the people want is very simple - they want an America as good as its promise."*

**Did you know?** Barbara was a fervent advocate for the Voting Rights Act.

## 18 MARCH
# Favianna Rodriguez
Artist and Activist

1978-Present, USA

Favianna Rodriguez is a contemporary American artist and activist whose work is a vibrant tapestry of social commentary and advocacy. Using bold colors and compelling imagery, Rodriguez's art confronts and challenges viewers on critical issues such as immigration, gender equality, racial justice, and climate change. Her approach to art is deeply intertwined with her activism, reflecting her belief in the transformative power of art as a tool for social change and public discourse.

Rodriguez's work often features strong, empowered figures and motifs drawn from nature and diverse cultural symbols, offering a visual language that speaks to the interconnectedness of human rights and environmental sustainability.

**Did you know?** Beyond her art, Favianna Rodriguez is a committed activist. She co-founded "CultureStrike," an organization that leverages the power of arts to promote immigrant rights.

## 19 MARCH

# Mother Jones

Fierce Labor and Community Organizer

1837-1930, USA

Born Mary Harris, "Mother" Jones was a fearless labor organizer, advocating for workers' rights, especially in the coal mining industry. Despite facing numerous arrests, she never wavered in her mission.

*"Pray for the dead and fight like hell for the living."*

**Did you know?** Mother Jones was once labeled "the most dangerous woman in America" due to her activism.

## 20 MARCH

# Patsy Mink

Advocate for Women's Rights and Education

1927-2002, USA

Patsy Mink, the first Asian-American woman elected to Congress, co-authored the landmark Title IX legislation, which prohibits gender-based discrimination in federally funded education.

*"It is easy enough to vote right and be consistently with the majority... but it is more often more important to be ahead of the majority."*

**Did you know?** The Title IX amendment was renamed the Patsy T. Mink Equal Opportunity in Education Act after her death.

## 21 MARCH

# Angela Merkel

The Iron Chancellor of Germany

1954-Present, Germany

Navigating the intricate world of politics, Angela Merkel emerged as Germany's first female Chancellor. Steering the country for over a decade, she's lauded for her pragmatic leadership, especially during Europe's financial crises.

> *"We Europeans truly have our fate in our own hands."*

**Did you know?** Angela Merkel holds a doctorate in quantum chemistry and worked as a research scientist until entering politics.

## 22 MARCH

# Jeannette Rankin
The First Woman in the U.S. Congress

1880-1973, USA

Breaking barriers, Jeannette Rankin became the first woman elected to the U.S. Congress in 1916. A lifelong pacifist, she was the only Congress member to vote against entering both World Wars.

*"I may be the first woman member of Congress, but I won't be the last."*

**Did you know?** Rankin's first term in Congress preceded the ratification of the 19th Amendment, granting women the right to vote.

## 23 MARCH

# Patricia Bath

Revolutionary Ophthalmologist

1942-2019, USA

Dr. Patricia Bath shattered glass ceilings, becoming the first African-American female doctor granted a medical patent. Her invention, the Laserphaco Probe, revolutionized cataract treatment worldwide.

*"Do not allow your mind to be imprisoned by majority thinking."*

**Did you know?** Bath co-founded the American Institute for the Prevention of Blindness.

## 24 MARCH

# Juliette Gordon Low
Founder of the Girl Scouts

1860-1927, USA

After meeting the founder of the Boy Scouts, Juliette Gordon Low was inspired to establish a similar organization for girls. In 1912, she founded the Girl Scouts, emphasizing outdoor activities, self-reliance, and service.

*"The work of today is the history of tomorrow, and we are its makers."*

**Did you know?** Despite her hearing impairment, Low remained active and enthusiastic about promoting the Girl Scouts.

## 25 MARCH

# Janet Reno

First Female U.S. Attorney General

1938-2016, USA

Sworn in under President Bill Clinton, Janet Reno was the first woman to serve as U.S. Attorney General. Her tenure, though occasionally controversial, saw her take on challenges from the Branch Davidian standoff to antitrust charges against Microsoft.

*"I'm not fancy. I'm what I appear to be."*

**Did you know?** Reno never lost a campaign and served as Attorney General for the entirety of Clinton's presidency.

## 26 MARCH

# Anacaona

Taino Cacique and Poet

1474-1503, Hispaniola (now Haiti and the Dominican Republic)

Anacaona, whose name means 'Golden Flower' in the Taino language, was a revered cacique (chief) and a cultural icon of the Taino people in Hispaniola, an island in the Caribbean now divided into Haiti and the Dominican Republic. As a leader, she was known not only for her political acumen but also for her artistic talents in poetry and song, which she used to preserve and celebrate Taino culture and history.

One of the most notable events in her life was the hosting of a large gathering of indigenous leaders, which was intended to be a peaceful assembly. However, the Spanish colonial authorities perceived this as a threat to their power. The tragic outcome of this gathering, where the Spanish betrayed and captured Anacaona, marked a significant moment in the history of resistance against colonial forces in the Americas.

**Did you know?** Anacaona was one of the earliest female rulers to resist European colonization in the New World.

## 27 MARCH

# Carmen Miranda
Brazilian Bombshell

1909-1955, Brazil

Emanating vibrant energy, Carmen Miranda was a Portuguese-born Brazilian samba singer, dancer, and actress. Her iconic fruit-hat image popularized Brazilian music and culture in the U.S.

> *"I say 20 words in English. I say money, money, money, and I say hot dog! I say yes, no and I say money, money, money and I say turkey sandwich and I say grape juice."*

**Did you know?** Miranda holds a Guinness World Record as the highest-paid actress in Hollywood in 1945.

## 28 MARCH

# Maud Stevens Wagner

America's First Female Tattoo Artist

1877-1961, USA

Beginning her tattooing journey at the 1904 World's Fair, Maud Stevens Wagner learned the hand-poked tattoo method, becoming America's first-known female tattoo artist. She also performed in circuses as an aerialist and contortionist.

**Did you know?** Maud often exchanged romantic letters with her husband in the form of tattoos.

## 29 MARCH

# Coco Chanel

Fashion Icon

1883-1971, France

Redefining women's fashion, Coco Chanel introduced comfortable elegance, replacing constricting corsets with jersey dresses and pearls. Her legacy, including the Chanel No. 5 perfume, persists as a symbol of luxury.

> *"In order to be irreplaceable, one must always be different."*

**Did you know?** Chanel's little black dress is considered a fashion staple, symbolizing sophistication and simplicity.

## 30 MARCH

# Queen Gudit
Ethiopian Jewish Queen

10th Century, Ethiopia

Queen Gudit, also known as Yodit or Judith, is a figure shrouded in legend and mystery in Ethiopian history. Rising to power in the 10th century, she is often depicted as a fierce and formidable ruler who led a series of revolts that significantly impacted the region's history. Her reign is notably marked by the destruction of churches and religious monuments, which has led to a mixed legacy.

To some, Gudit is remembered as a ruthless destroyer who brought about the end of the Aksumite Kingdom, a major trading empire in the Horn of Africa. However, others view her as a symbol of resistance and a revolutionary figure who challenged the established religious and political order of her time. This duality in her legacy reflects the complexities of historical narratives, especially when viewed through different cultural and religious lenses.

**Did you know?** Queen Gudit's rule is considered a significant, albeit enigmatic, chapter in Ethiopian history, and she is often cited as a precursor to the rise of the Zagwe dynasty.

## 31 MARCH

# Queen Amanirenas of Kush
### Kandake Warrior Queen

1st Century BCE, Kingdom of Kush
(located in what is now Sudan)

Queen Amanirenas, a formidable Kandake (queen) of the ancient Kingdom of Kush, is celebrated for her extraordinary leadership and military acumen. During the 1st century BCE, when the Roman Empire sought to expand its territories into Kushite lands, Queen Amanirenas stood as a bulwark against these incursions.

Her reign was marked by a fierce resistance against Roman invasions, showcasing not only her tactical prowess but also her unyielding bravery. Amanirenas, who was partially blind, led her armies with remarkable skill and determination. Her fearless leadership in battles, including the well-documented campaign against Roman Egypt, earned her a reputation as a formidable warrior queen.

After years of relentless warfare, Queen Amanirenas negotiated a peace treaty with Rome. This treaty was a significant achievement as it ensured the sovereignty and autonomy of the Kushite Kingdom, a feat that few leaders of her time could accomplish. Under this treaty, Kush was exempted from paying tribute to

Rome, marking a rare instance of the Roman Empire conceding to a smaller power.

**Did you know?** Kandake, a title for Kushite queens, symbolizes not only their royal status but also their role as "queen mother" or "great woman," reflecting the matrilineal aspects of Kushite society.

# APRIL

## 1 APRIL

# Jane Austen

Celebrated English Novelist

1775-1817, England

Delving into the British landed gentry of the late 18th century, Jane Austen's novels, including "Pride and Prejudice" and "Sense and Sensibility," provide timeless insights into society, relationships, and individual aspirations.

> *"I declare after all there is no enjoyment like reading! How much sooner one tires of anything than of a book!"*

**Did you know?** Jane Austen's identity as a published author was a well-guarded secret during her lifetime, with her books initially appearing as being written "by a lady."

## 2 APRIL

# Marie Curie
Pioneer in Radioactivity

1867-1934, Poland/France

A trailblazer in science, Marie Curie was the first woman to win a Nobel Prize and remains the only person to win Nobel Prizes in two different scientific fields, Physics and Chemistry. Her discoveries of radium and polonium revolutionized cancer treatments.

*"Nothing in life is to be feared, it is only to be understood. Now is the time to understand more, so that we may fear less."*

**Did you know?** Curie's research papers from the 1890s are still considered too radioactive to handle without protection.

## 3 APRIL

# Dolley Madison

America's Beloved First Lady

1768-1849, USA

As First Lady, Dolley Madison defined the role with her social graces, diplomacy, and resilience. During the War of 1812, she famously saved George Washington's portrait from the burning White House.

*"I am enjoying fine health and am more and more pleased with my journey."*

**Did you know?** Dolley was known for her delectable snack, now famous as 'Dolley Madison Cakes'.

## 4 APRIL

# Mirabai

Devotional Poetess and Saint

1498-1557, India

A Rajput princess turned saint, Mirabai dedicated her life to the worship of Lord Krishna. Her bhajans (devotional songs) expressed her deep spiritual fervor and longing for the divine.

**Did you know?** It's believed that Mirabai miraculously survived many attempts on her life due to her unwavering faith.

## 5 APRIL

# Nancy Wake

WWII's Most Decorated Servicewoman

1912-2011, New Zealand/Australia

This fierce resistance fighter, known as the "White Mouse" by the Nazis, was a leading figure in the French Resistance during WWII. Nancy Wake's exploits made her Gestapo's most-wanted person.

*"Freedom is the only thing worth living for. While I was doing that work, I used to think it didn't matter if I died, because without freedom there was no point in living."*

**Did you know?** Wake once killed an SS sentry with her bare hands to prevent an alarm from being raised.

6 APRIL

# Harriet Jacobs
Advocate Against Slavery

1813-1897, USA

Born into slavery, Harriet Jacobs penned "Incidents in the Life of a Slave Girl," highlighting the sexual harassment and abuse endured by female slaves. Her narrative became instrumental in the abolitionist movement.

**Did you know?** Jacobs hid in a tiny attic space for seven years to escape her abusive master and protect her children.

## 7 APRIL

# Misty Copeland
Pioneering Ballerina

1982-Present, USA

Misty Copeland leapt into history as the first African American Female Principal Dancer with the prestigious American Ballet Theatre. She's an embodiment of breaking barriers in the classical dance world.

> *"You can do anything you want, even if you are being told negative things. Stay strong and find motivation."*

**Did you know?** Copeland began ballet training at the late age of 13, which is considered old in the ballet world.

## 8 APRIL
# Billie Jean King
Tennis Legend and Equal Rights Advocate

1943-Present, USA

Billie Jean King's contribution to tennis and women's rights goes far beyond her impressive record on the court. Her victory over Bobby Riggs in the famed "Battle of the Sexes" match symbolized the fight for gender equality, transcending sports and entering the broader cultural discourse. King's advocacy extended to issues like equal pay and LGBTQ+ rights, making her a pivotal figure in the women's movement of the 20th century.

*"Champions keep playing until they get it right."* –
*Billie Jean King*

**Did you know?** King's 39 Grand Slam titles include singles, doubles, and mixed doubles championships, showcasing her versatility and dominance in the sport.

## 9 APRIL

# Coretta Scott King
Civil Rights Leader and Philanthropist

1927-2006, USA

While often recognized as the wife of Martin Luther King Jr., Coretta was a monumental figure in the civil rights movement in her own right, advocating for racial and economic justice.

*"Hate is too great a burden to bear. It injures the hater more than it injures the hated."*

**Did you know?** Coretta played a crucial role in making Martin Luther King Jr.'s birthday a national holiday.

## 10 APRIL

# Queen Sorghaghtani of the Mongol Empire
Influential Regent

1190-1252, Mongolia

Queen Sorghaghtani, mother to four Mongol Great Khans including Kublai Khan, was a pivotal figure in the Mongol Empire. A Nestorian Christian in a predominantly Buddhist and Shamanist society, she was renowned for her wisdom, diplomatic skills, and foresight. Under her guidance, her sons became some of the most significant rulers of the Mongol Empire, expanding its reach and influence. She was a proponent of religious tolerance and played a crucial role in the administration of the empire, ensuring its stability and growth during transitional periods.

**Did you know?** Marco Polo referred to her as the most influential woman of her age, a testament to her remarkable impact on Mongol politics and the broader Eurasian history.

## 11 APRIL

# Katherine Switzer
Marathon Pioneer

1947-Present, USA

Switzer made history as the first woman to officially run the Boston Marathon, even as officials tried to physically stop her, proving women could tackle the distance.

*"If you are losing faith in human nature, go out and watch a marathon."*

**Did you know?** Her 1967 Boston Marathon bib number, 261, has become a symbol of women's empowerment in sports.

## 12 APRIL

# Fatima al-Fihri

Founder of the World's Oldest University

800-880, Morocco

Fatima al-Fihri's founding of Al-Qarawiyyin University in Fez, Morocco, marks a significant milestone in the history of education and academia. Her dedication to knowledge and learning established a center that would influence scholars and thinkers for centuries to come. Al-Fihri's vision was revolutionary, creating an institution that welcomed students to engage in a wide array of subjects, from theology to astronomy.

**Did you know?** Al-Qarawiyyin University, recognized by UNESCO and the Guinness World Records, is a testament to the rich academic and cultural heritage of the Islamic world in the medieval period.

## 13 APRIL

# Hurrem Sultan

Powerful Consort of the Ottoman Empire

1502-1558, Ottoman Empire

Also known as Roxelana, Hurrem Sultan rose from being a slave to becoming the chief consort of Sultan Suleiman the Magnificent. Her influence on Ottoman politics and culture was unparalleled.

**Did you know?** Hurrem Sultan commissioned several major architectural projects, including mosques, schools, and hospitals.

## 14 APRIL

# Valentina Tereshkova

First Woman in Space

1937-Present, Russia

In 1963, aboard Vostok 6, Valentina Tereshkova became the first woman to journey into space. This cosmonaut's mission lasted almost three days, and she orbited Earth 48 times.

> *"Once you've been in space, you appreciate how small and fragile the Earth is."*

**Did you know?** Tereshkova volunteered for a one-way trip to Mars, showing her indomitable spirit.

## 15 APRIL

# Alice Paul

Suffragist and Women's Rights Advocate

1885-1977, USA

Alice Paul dedicated her life to women's rights. She played a key role in the 19th Amendment, which granted U.S. women the right to vote, and later penned the Equal Rights Amendment.

*"I never doubted that equal rights was the right direction. Most reforms, most problems are complicated. But to me there is nothing complicated about ordinary equality."*

**Did you know?** Paul was imprisoned for her suffragist activities and organized hunger strikes inside the jail.

## 16 APRIL

# Virginia Woolf

Innovative English Writer

1882-1941, England

A literary giant of the 20th century, Virginia Woolf is celebrated for pioneering modernist literary techniques. With novels like "Mrs Dalloway" and "To the Lighthouse", Woolf beautifully captured the innermost thoughts and emotions of her characters.

*"For most of history, Anonymous was a woman."*

**Did you know?** Woolf was a key figure in the Bloomsbury Group, an influential group of writers, intellectuals, and artists.

## 17 APRIL

# Rosalyn Sussman Yalow
Nobel Laureate in Medicine

1921-2011, USA

A pioneering medical physicist, Yalow co-developed the radioimmunoassay technique, revolutionizing endocrinology by allowing scientists to measure minute amounts of biological substances in the body.

*"We cannot expect in the immediate future that all women who seek it will achieve full equality of opportunity."*

**Did you know?** Yalow was the second woman ever to win a Nobel Prize in Physiology or Medicine.

## 365 INSPIRING WOMEN

### 18 APRIL

# Junko Tabei

First Woman to Summit Everest

1939-2016, Japan

Tabei made history in 1975 when she reached the peak of Mount Everest. She didn't stop there; Tabei became the first woman to climb the Seven Summits, the tallest peak on each continent.

*"Technique and ability alone do not get you to the top; it is the willpower that is the most important."*

**Did you know?** After Everest, Tabei founded an environmental group to clean up waste from mountainous regions.

## 19 APRIL

# Catherine de' Medici
Influential Queen of France

1519-1589, France

Catherine de' Medici, an Italian noblewoman who became the queen consort of France, was a masterful political strategist. During her time as queen consort and regent, she navigated the complexities of the French court, particularly during the turbulent times of the religious wars between Catholics and Huguenots. Her influence extended to cultural aspects as well, including gastronomy and the arts, and she is often credited with enhancing the sophistication of the French court.

**Did you know?** Catherine's introduction of the fork from Italy to France was part of a broader influence she had on French dining and culture, which continues to be felt today.

## 20 APRIL

# Isabella Bird
Intrepid Explorer and Writer

1831-1904, England

An adventurer at heart, Bird traversed continents from the Americas to Asia, detailing her travels in several books. She was the first woman inducted into the Royal Geographical Society.

*"Hawaii is paradise born of fire."*

**Did you know?** Despite suffering from chronic health issues, Bird traveled the world on horseback, canoe, and even on foot.

## 21 APRIL

# Susan B. Anthony

Champion of Women's Rights

1820-1906, USA

A fierce advocate for women's suffrage, Anthony was instrumental in the early efforts to secure voting rights for women. Her dedication led to the 19th Amendment, granting US women the right to vote.

*"Failure is impossible."*

**Did you know?** Anthony was once fined $100 for voting illegally in the 1872 presidential election. She never paid the fine.

## 22 APRIL

# Ada Yonath

Crystallography Trailblazer

1939-Present, Israel

Ada Yonath, a pioneering Israeli crystallographer, made significant contributions to our understanding of the molecular structure of ribosomes — essential for protein synthesis in cells. Her research, which culminated in the Nobel Prize in Chemistry, has had profound implications in the medical field, particularly in the understanding and treatment of antibiotic resistance. Yonath's work is notable not only for its scientific brilliance but also for paving the way for women in a field traditionally dominated by men.

*"I was not aware of any gender-specific encouragement or discouragement in my family or school. I was a curious child, interested in how things work, and my environment responded positively to this." - Ada Yonath*

**Did you know?** Ada Yonath's achievement as the first Israeli woman to win a Nobel in the sciences is a landmark in the annals of scientific discovery and gender equality in the field.

## 23 APRIL

# Rosa Parks

Mother of the Civil Rights Movement

1913-2005, USA

By refusing to give up her bus seat in Montgomery, Alabama, Parks sparked a boycott that became a pivotal event in the fight against racial segregation in America.

> *"I would like to be remembered as a person who wanted to be free... so other people would also be free."*

**Did you know?** Rosa Parks wasn't the first to resist bus segregation, but her act was the catalyst for widespread change.

## 24 APRIL

# Wilma Mankiller

First Female Principal Chief of
the Cherokee Nation

1945-2010, USA

Wilma Mankiller's tenure as the first female Principal Chief of the Cherokee Nation was marked by significant progress in education, healthcare, and governance. Her leadership revitalized the Cherokee Nation, focusing on self-reliance and community development. Mankiller's advocacy for Native American rights and her efforts to improve the socio-economic status of her people have left a lasting impact on the Cherokee Nation and serve as an inspiration for indigenous leadership worldwide.

*"The secret of our success is that we never, never give up." - Wilma Mankiller*

**Did you know?** The name 'Mankiller' reflects a traditional Cherokee military rank, symbolizing strength and leadership, and is unrelated to the English term "man-killer."

## 25 APRIL

# Anais Nin

Visionary Diarist and Writer

1903-1977, France/USA

Through her diaries and fiction, Nin delved into themes of identity, love, and femininity. Her works, including "Delta of Venus", remain influential in feminist literature.

*"We do not see things as they are, we see them as we are."*

**Did you know?** Nin began her diary at age 11 and continued it for over 60 years.

## 26 APRIL

# Maria Montessori
Revolutionary Educator

1870-1952, Italy

Montessori's innovative teaching philosophies emphasized hands-on, individualized learning, radically transforming early childhood education around the world.

> *"Education is a natural process carried out by the child and is not acquired by listening to words but by experiences in the environment."*

**Did you know?** Montessori was the first woman in Italy to earn a medical degree.

## 27 APRIL

# Marie Tharp

Cartographer of the Ocean Floor

1920-2006, USA

Working in a male-dominated field, Tharp meticulously mapped the ocean floor, revealing the Mid-Atlantic Ridge and providing evidence for the theory of continental drift.

**Did you know?** For a time, Tharp's discoveries were dismissed as "girl talk" by some male scientists.

## 28 APRIL
# Mahalia Jackson
Queen of Gospel

1911-1972, USA

Jackson's powerful voice and soul-stirring performances helped popularize gospel music. Beyond music, she was a fervent advocate for civil rights.

*"If you sing gospel you can't do anything wrong."*

**Did you know?** Jackson sang "I've Been 'Buked, and I've Been Scorned" just before Martin Luther King Jr.'s "I Have a Dream" speech.

## 29 APRIL

# Toypurina

Native American Revolutionary

1760-1799, Tongva Nation, California

Toypurina, a revered medicine woman of the Tongva Nation, emerged as a symbol of resistance against Spanish colonial rule in California. She led a daring rebellion to protect her people's land, culture, and way of life from Spanish encroachment. Her courage and defiance in the face of colonial powers have made her a legendary figure in Native American history. Toypurina's story, embodying the spirit of resistance and resilience, continues to inspire through adaptations in plays and literature.

**Did you know?** Toypurina's legacy is celebrated in various forms of art and literature, serving as a powerful reminder of the indigenous struggle and resistance in North America.

## 30 APRIL

# Grace Hopper
Computer Science Pioneer

1906-1992, USA

A mathematician and rear admiral in the U.S. Navy, Hopper was instrumental in the development of early computer programming. She's best known for her work on the first compiler.

*"The most dangerous phrase in the language is, 'We've always done it this way.'"*

**Did you know?** A minor "computer bug" became the term for a software glitch after Hopper found an actual moth causing issues in a machine.

365 INSPIRING WOMEN

# MAY

## 1 MAY

# George Eliot

The Pen Name Behind Literary Masterpieces

1819-1880, England

Mary Ann Evans, known by her pen name George Eliot, is one of the leading novelists of the Victorian era. She chose a male pseudonym to ensure her works would be taken seriously in an age where male authors dominated the literary world. Eliot's novels, including "Middlemarch" and "Silas Marner", are celebrated for their realism, psychological insight, and detailed portrayal of rural life. Her ability to delve deep into the human psyche made her works timeless and universally relatable.

*"It is never too late to be what you might have been."*

**Did you know?** George Eliot's real identity remained a mystery until she publicly acknowledged it in 1857.

## 2 MAY

# Mary Edwards Walker

Pioneering Surgeon and Women's Rights Advocate

1832-1919, USA

Dr. Mary Edwards Walker remains the only woman to have received the Medal of Honor, America's highest military honor. A surgeon during the Civil War, she frequently crossed battle lines to treat the wounded from both sides. Apart from her medical pursuits, she was a fierce advocate for women's rights, often wearing male attire and getting arrested for it.

*"I have always believed that the Almighty made both men and women equal."*

**Did you know?** Walker's Medal of Honor was revoked in 1917, only to be restored posthumously in 1977.

## 3 MAY

# Dorothy Vaughan

NASA's Trailblazing Mathematician

1910-2008, USA

As one of NASA's human "computers," Dorothy Vaughan played an instrumental role in America's race to space. Despite racial and gender barriers, she became the first African-American supervisor at the National Advisory Committee for Aeronautics (NACA), NASA's predecessor. Her leadership and expertise in FORTRAN made vital contributions to the success of early space missions.

*"Know your own self-worth and take pride in your work."*

**Did you know?** The film "Hidden Figures" spotlights Vaughan's contributions to the space program.

## 4 MAY

# Indira Gandhi
India's First Female Prime Minister

1917-1984, India

As the first woman Prime Minister of India, Indira Gandhi left an indelible mark on the world's largest democracy. Serving four terms, she navigated India through numerous challenges, both domestic and international. Her tenure saw important reforms but also faced criticisms. Her powerful leadership style and political savvy make her a figure of both reverence and controversy.

*"My grandfather once told me that there were two kinds of people: those who do the work and those who take the credit."*

**Did you know?** Indira wasn't related to Mahatma Gandhi, despite sharing the same surname.

## 5 MAY

# Agnes Macphail

Canada's First Female Member of Parliament

1890-1954, Canada

Breaking barriers in Canadian politics, Agnes Macphail became the first woman elected to the Canadian House of Commons. She fought for prison reform, disarmament, and minority rights, showcasing her passion for justice. Her tenacity and vision paved the way for future female politicians in Canada.

*"Never apologize. Never explain. Just get the thing done, and let them howl."*

**Did you know?** Macphail was also one of the first two women elected to the Ontario legislature.

## 6 MAY

# Edith Cavell
Heroic World War I Nurse

1865-1915, England

Working in German-occupied Belgium during World War I, Edith Cavell was a British nurse who saved soldiers from both sides without any discrimination. She also helped over 200 Allied soldiers escape from German-occupied Belgium, for which she was arrested, tried, and executed.

*"Patriotism is not enough. I must have no hatred or bitterness towards anyone."*

**Did you know?** Edith became a symbol of selfless dedication during and after the War.

## 7 MAY

# Micaela Bastidas

Unsung Heroine of Peruvian Independence

1744-1781, Peru

Often overshadowed by her husband, Tupac Amaru II, Micaela Bastidas was a key figure in Peru's rebellion against Spanish colonial rule. Her strategic insights, leadership, and unwavering spirit made her a formidable force in the uprising.

*"For freedom, I'd sacrifice even life itself."*

**Did you know?** Micaela is often hailed as the "Pioneering Woman of Independence" in South American history.

## 8 MAY

# Frida Kahlo

Mexico's Iconic Painter

1907-1954, Mexico

Frida Kahlo, overcoming immense personal challenges including polio and a devastating bus accident, transformed her experiences of pain, passion, and resilience into vibrant art. Her works, characterized by bold colors and a surrealistic style, delve deep into her emotional landscape, reflecting her life's struggles and her rich Mexican heritage. "The Two Fridas," one of her most famous paintings, is a poignant exploration of her complex identity and experiences. Kahlo's art transcends the personal, resonating universally with themes of suffering, strength, and the human condition.

*"I paint my own reality." - Frida Kahlo*

**Did you know?** Kahlo's deep affinity for animals was evident in her diverse menagerie of pets, including dogs, deer, and monkeys, which often featured in her art and provided companionship throughout her life.

## 9 MAY

# Eleanor of Aquitaine
Europe's Most Powerful Duchess

1122-1204, France and England

From Queen of France to Queen of England, Eleanor of Aquitaine was one of the most influential women of the Middle Ages. Her vast territories in southwestern France made her Europe's foremost duchess. Beyond politics, she was a patron of literature and the arts.

*"One must live, after all."*

**Did you know?** Eleanor went on the Second Crusade, a rarity for women of her time.

## 10 MAY
# Empress Xiaozhuang
The Wise Matriarch of the Qing Dynasty

1613-1688, China

Empress Xiaozhuang, originally named Bumbutai, was a significant and influential figure during the early years of the Qing dynasty. Not born into royalty, her rise to power was marked by wisdom, resilience, and shrewdness. Initially a consort, Xiaozhuang later played a crucial role in the political landscape of China, ensuring the success of both her son and grandson as emperors.

*"In times of turbulence, a throne becomes a heavy burden."*

**Did you know?** Empress Xiaozhuang wasn't Chinese. She was a Borjigit Mongol, and her cultural background had a significant influence on Qing dynasty policies.

## 11 MAY

# Ida B. Wells

Journalist and Civil Rights Crusader

1862-1931, USA

Ida B. Wells was an African-American journalist, abolitionist, and feminist. She led an anti-lynching crusade in the 1890s and went on to establish several civil rights organizations. Her fierce and fearless commitment to justice, especially concerning violence against Black people, made her a significant figure in the early civil rights movement.

*"The way to right wrongs is to turn the light of truth upon them."*

**Did you know?** Wells started her activism after being thrown out of a first-class train carriage, even though she had a ticket. She sued the railroad and won, although the decision was later overturned.

## 12 MAY

# Winona LaDuke
Indigenous Environmental Activist

1959-Present, USA

Winona LaDuke, an Ojibwe Native American, is a passionate advocate for indigenous rights and environmental issues. With dual Harvard degrees, she returned to the White Earth Ojibwe Reservation, working tirelessly to recover tribal lands. Later, as co-founder of the Indigenous Women's Network and the Honor the Earth campaign, LaDuke cemented her place as a frontline activist against projects like the Dakota Access Pipeline.

*"Someone needs to explain to me why wanting clean drinking water makes you an activist, and why proposing to destroy water with chemical warfare doesn't make a corporation a terrorist."*

**Did you know?** LaDuke ran for the U.S. vice-presidency twice alongside Ralph Nader.

## 13 MAY

# Grace O'Malley
## The Pirate Queen of Ireland

1530-1603, Ireland

Braving the tempestuous seas, Grace O'Malley, or Gráinne Mhaol, emerged as a dominant force along Ireland's west coast. Reputed as a pirate, chieftain, and defender of her territory and people, she challenged the English crown's encroachment, famously meeting with Queen Elizabeth I to negotiate terms.

*"We have but one life to live, and during it, I wish to live as a free person."*

**Did you know?** O'Malley's encounter with Queen Elizabeth was remarkable as both communicated in Latin.

## 14 MAY

# Mary Lou Williams
The Lady Who Swings the Band

1910-1981, USA

From the heart of the jazz era, Mary Lou Williams emerged as a pianist, composer, and arranger extraordinaire. Transcending the early blues, through swing, bebop, and beyond, Williams never ceased innovating. She played with and mentored some of the biggest names in jazz, leaving a legacy that's still felt today.

*"I did it, because it was supposed to be impossible for a woman to write for a band, that's why I did it."*

**Did you know?** Williams organized free Saturday morning lessons for young musicians, furthering their careers.

## 15 MAY

# Oprah Winfrey

Media Mogul and Philanthropist

1954-Present, USA

Oprah Winfrey's journey, from a tumultuous childhood to becoming a media titan, is a testament to perseverance. Her daytime talk show revolutionized the format, becoming a platform for personal stories, societal issues, and global outreach. Beyond television, she's an influential producer, actress, and philanthropist, particularly for education and health causes.

*"Turn your wounds into wisdom."*

**Did you know?** Oprah's Book Club has catapulted many authors to fame and increased literary appreciation.

## 16 MAY

# Clara Barton

Founder of the American Red Cross

1821-1912, USA

Throughout the Civil War, Clara Barton risked her life to bring supplies and support to soldiers in the field. Her tireless dedication led her to create the American Red Cross, mirroring the International Red Cross's principles. Clara's humanitarian vision ensures that, even today, people receive aid during disasters.

*"I may be compelled to face danger, but never fear it, and while our soldiers can stand and fight, I can stand and feed and nurse them."*

**Did you know?** Clara was also a teacher and patent clerk before her Red Cross endeavors.

## 17 MAY

# Charlotte Forten Grimké

Abolitionist and Educator

1837-1914, USA

As a freeborn black woman in Philadelphia, Charlotte Forten Grimké was educated and passionate about abolishing slavery. She taught freedmen on South Carolina's Sea Islands, wrote influential diaries about her experiences, and later, as a Grimké through marriage, became part of a leading abolitionist family.

*"To enlighten, elevate, and educate our people is the only sure way to save them from degradation and vice."*

**Did you know?** Charlotte's diaries are among the few documenting African-American life during the Civil War.

## 18 MAY

# Charlotte Brontë
### Author of 'Jane Eyre'

1816-1855, England

Raised on the windswept moors of Yorkshire, Charlotte Brontë and her siblings created rich fantasy worlds that would fuel their literary imaginations. Charlotte's masterpiece, "Jane Eyre," stands out for its groundbreaking approach, blending gothic elements with profound psychological insight. The novel's strong, independent female protagonist was a significant departure from the norm and helped lay the groundwork for modern feminist literature.

*"I am no bird; and no net ensnares me: I am a free human being with an independent will." - Charlotte Brontë*

**Did you know?** Charlotte initially published "Jane Eyre" under the male pseudonym Currer Bell, challenging the gender biases of the Victorian literary world.

## 19 MAY

# Artemisia I of Caria
Warrior Queen of Halicarnassus

5th century BCE, Ancient Greece

Artemisia I of Caria, a queen and naval commander, distinguished herself in the Persian Wars, particularly in the Battle of Salamis. Her strategic acumen and courage as the only woman in King Xerxes' war council earned her a formidable reputation. She navigated the complex dynamics of power and warfare with finesse, often outsmarting her Greek adversaries and leaving a legacy as one of the most remarkable women of ancient history.

**Did you know?** Artemisia's tactical retreat at Salamis, though on the losing side, was a strategic decision that preserved her fleet and demonstrated her military prudence.

## 20 MAY
# Chimamanda Ngozi Adichie
Celebrated Nigerian Novelist

1977-Present, Nigeria

Chimamanda Ngozi Adichie's voice has become synonymous with modern African literature. Born in Nigeria, she has penned multiple novels, including the acclaimed "Half of a Yellow Sun". A vocal advocate for women's rights and African identity, her work weaves complex tales of post-colonialism, gender, and varying human experiences.

*"Culture does not make people. People make culture. If it is true that the full humanity of women is not our culture, then we can and must make it our culture."*

**Did you know?** Chimamanda was mentioned in Beyoncé's song "Flawless", amplifying her feminist views to a global audience.

## 21 MAY

# Hélène Cixous

Pioneer of Écriture Féminine

1937-Present, Algeria/France

A prolific thinker, Hélène Cixous proposed the groundbreaking idea of 'Écriture Féminine' – a distinct feminine style of writing. This French literary critic, poet, playwright, and philosopher championed a unique form of feminist criticism, urging women to break from male-structured language norms.

*"I felt myself to be man and woman, muscle and velvet, in and out of my skin."*

**Did you know?** Hélène's multicultural Algerian Jewish background deeply influenced her work on identity.

## 22 MAY
# Rabi'a al-Adawiyya
Pioneering Sufi Mystic

717-801, Basra, Iraq

Rabi'a, often considered the first female Sufi saint, played a foundational role in shaping the Sufi tradition, emphasizing love and devotion to the Divine over ritualistic practices. Her poetry reflects deep spiritual introspection and a passionate longing for union with the Divine.

*"In love, nothing exists between heart and heart."*

**Did you know?** Rabi'a introduced the concept of pure love, claiming she loved God for God's own essence, not out of fear of hell or hope of paradise.

## 23 MAY

# Shajar al-Durr

Egypt's Trailblazing Ruler

1220-1257, Egypt

Born as a slave, Shajar al-Durr's intelligence and charisma saw her rise to become the wife of Sultan As-Salih Ayyub and later, Egypt's ruler. Her reign marked the start of the Mamluk era. Formidable and clever, she played a pivotal role in the Seventh Crusade, contributing to the capture of King Louis IX of France.

*"A ruler's strength isn't in their lineage but their ability."*

**Did you know?** Upon her husband's death, Shajar cleverly hid the news to ensure a smooth transition of power, showcasing her strategic acumen.

## 24 MAY

# Emma Goldman

Fierce Advocate of Free Thought

1869-1940, Lithuania/USA

Emma Goldman, a trailblazing activist and anarchist, championed a wide array of causes including women's rights, free speech, and social reform. Her passionate advocacy and eloquent oratory made her a prominent figure in the anarchist movement. Goldman's life was marked by constant travel, spreading her revolutionary ideas, and her arrests were a testament to her commitment to her beliefs and her challenge to societal norms.

*Quote: "If I can't dance, I don't want to be part of your revolution." - Emma Goldman*

**Did you know?** Goldman's radical views, especially her opposition to conscription, led to her deportation from the United States, a country she had called home for decades.

## 25 MAY

# Mary Pickford

Hollywood's First Superstar

1892-1979, Canada/USA

Starting in silent films, Mary Pickford soon became a force to reckon with in Hollywood, co-founding United Artists. Known as "America's Sweetheart," she was instrumental in the shift from silent films to talkies and had immense influence during the early days of cinema.

*"If you have made mistakes...there is always another chance for you...you may have a fresh start any moment you choose."*

**Did you know?** Mary was a founding member of the Academy of Motion Picture Arts and Sciences, which hosts the Oscars.

## 26 MAY

# Margaret Thatcher

Britain's First Female Prime Minister

1925-2013, United Kingdom

Margaret Thatcher, often referred to as the 'Iron Lady', was the UK's first female prime minister and the longest-serving British PM of the 20th century. Known for her strong conservative policies and formidable character, she reshaped the nation's economic landscape and left a profound mark on British politics.

*"If you want something said, ask a man; if you want something done, ask a woman."*

**Did you know?** Margaret started her career in chemistry and was part of a team that developed the first soft ice cream.

## 27 MAY

# Amina, Queen of Zazzau
### Warrior Queen of Nigeria

1533-1610, Zazzau (Now Nigeria)

Queen Amina was one of the greatest African queens in recorded history. As a military leader and expansionist, she fortified her city, expanded her kingdom, and established Zazzau as a dominant regional power. Her reign was marked by both prosperity and extensive conquests.

*"A woman's strength isn't just in her heart, but in her command and determination."*

**Did you know?** Some city walls, known as 'Amina's Walls', are attributed to her and still stand in parts of Nigeria today.

## 28 MAY

# Audrey Hepburn
Hollywood's Elegant Star and Humanitarian

1929-1993, Belgium/USA

Audrey Hepburn, with her grace and beauty, became a Hollywood legend, starring in classics like "Breakfast at Tiffany's." But beyond the camera, she dedicated much of her life to humanitarian work, especially for UNICEF, focusing on children suffering from hunger worldwide.

> *"As you grow older, you will discover that you have two hands, one for helping yourself, the other for helping others."*

**Did you know?** Audrey trained as a ballet dancer before her film career took off.

## 29 MAY

# Flannery O'Connor
### Master of Southern Gothic Fiction

1925-1964, USA

Flannery O'Connor is best known for her distinctive Southern Gothic style that blends the grotesque with humor to explore themes of faith, redemption, and grace. Her stories, rich in symbolism, present characters facing moral and spiritual dilemmas.

*"The truth does not change according to our ability to stomach it."*

**Did you know?** Despite her short life, Flannery's work has left a lasting impression on modern literature.

## 30 MAY

# Gertrude Ederle

First Woman to Swim the English Channel

1905-2003, USA

In 1926, Gertrude Ederle did what no woman had done before: she swam the English Channel. Not only did she achieve this remarkable feat, but she also beat the men's record, making waves in sports history.

*"When someone tells me something can't be done, that's when I do it."*

**Did you know?** Gertrude wore motorcycle goggles sealed with paraffin to keep the saltwater out during her historic swim.

## 31 MAY

# Simone de Beauvoir

Philosophical Pillar of Feminism

1908-1986, France

Simone de Beauvoir, a philosopher, writer, and social theorist, is best known for "The Second Sex," a detailed analysis of women's oppression. Her work laid the groundwork for contemporary feminism, addressing existentialism and the human condition.

*"One is not born, but rather becomes, a woman."*

**Did you know?** Simone had a lifelong relationship with philosopher Jean-Paul Sartre, but they never married, challenging societal norms.

# JUNE

## 1 JUNE

# Wilma Rudolph
Olympic Champion Sprinter

1940-1994, USA

Born prematurely and stricken by polio, Wilma was told she might never walk again. Yet, through sheer determination and a family's support, not only did she walk but she sprinted, all the way to three Olympic gold medals in 1960, becoming the fastest woman in the world. From segregated Clarksville, Tennessee, Wilma's victories brought attention to racial divisions and she became instrumental in the desegregation of her hometown.

*"Never underestimate the power of dreams and the influence of the human spirit."*

**Did you know?** Despite her fame, Wilma insisted that her homecoming parade and banquet be integrated, the first racially integrated events in Clarksville.

## 2 JUNE
# Margaret Hamilton
Pioneer of Software Engineering

1936-Present, USA

Margaret led the team that developed the onboard flight software for NASA's Apollo missions, including the historic Apollo 11 moon landing. Her groundbreaking work and the term she coined, "software engineering," forever changed technology.

*"Our software was everywhere. Every string of code, we were intimately involved with."*

**Did you know?** A minor error during the Apollo 11 landing was corrected in real-time, thanks to Margaret's rigorous testing and foresight.

## 3 JUNE

# Sylvia Plath

Poet, Novelist, and Short Story Writer

1932-1963, USA

A gifted and troubled artist, Sylvia is best known for her novel "The Bell Jar" and her profound poetry. She confronted themes of identity, family, and mental illness with vivid imagery. Despite facing many personal struggles, her works remain a testament to the complexities of the human psyche.

*"I can never read all the books I want; I can never be all the people I want and live all the lives I want."*

**Did you know?** Sylvia was an accomplished artist and her drawings were published posthumously.

## 4 JUNE
# Elizabeth Garewrett Anderson
Britain's First Female Doctor

1836-1917, England

Battling gender norms, Elizabeth became the UK's first qualified female physician and surgeon. Refused entry into medical school, she studied privately and passed exams, leading her to open a hospital for women, run by women. She was a torchbearer for future female medics.

*"My strength and my wish lie in medicine."*

**Did you know?** Elizabeth inspired her younger sister, Millicent Garrett Fawcett, a key suffragist leader.

## 5 JUNE

# Alice Guy-Blaché
First Female Filmmaker

1873-1968, France/USA

Beginning her career as a secretary, Alice saw the potential in cinema and made one of the first-ever narrative films. She founded her own studio and produced over 1,000 films, many addressing social issues, but was often overlooked in male-dominated industry narratives.

> *"There is nothing connected with the staging of a motion picture that a woman cannot do as easily as a man."*

**Did you know?** Alice's films were some of the first to have synchronized sound.

## 6 JUNE

# Caroline Herschel
Astronomer Extraordinaire

1750-1848, Germany/England

From a singer in Germany to an astronomer in England, Caroline discovered several comets and contributed significantly to the field. Working with her brother, William Herschel, she became the first woman to be paid for her scientific work.

*"I was never in the whole course of my life at a play, ball, or assembly... music was the order of the day."*

**Did you know?** Caroline meticulously cataloged and confirmed thousands of stars during her career.

## 7 JUNE

# Nina Simone

Iconic Singer and Civil Rights Activist

1933-2003, USA

Blending classical, jazz, blues, and R&B, Nina Simone's deep, resounding voice became a soundtrack for Civil Rights. Beyond her musical genius, she used her platform to advocate for racial equality, penning protest songs.

*"I tell you what freedom is to me: No fear!"*

**Did you know?** Nina aspired to be a concert pianist and attended Julliard School of Music briefly.

## 8 JUNE
# Zenobia
Warrior Queen of Palmyra

240-275, Palmyra, Roman Syria

Bold and strategic, Queen Zenobia challenged the Roman Empire's might. Leading her army, she expanded Palmyra's empire, and her reign became legendary, symbolizing resistance against oppression.

**Did you know?** Zenobia claimed to be a descendant of Cleopatra, amplifying her link to power and resistance.

## 9 JUNE

# Tu Youyou

Nobel Prize-winning Pharmacologist

1930-Present, China

In a relentless quest to find a cure for malaria, Chinese pharmacologist Tu Youyou turned to ancient wisdom and modern science. Her discovery of artemisinin, derived from the sweet wormwood plant, has saved millions of lives worldwide. Tu's meticulous research, which involved delving into centuries-old Chinese medical texts and employing innovative extraction methods, led to this groundbreaking advancement in medical science. Her work exemplifies a remarkable blend of traditional knowledge and contemporary scientific methods.

> *"The award is recognition for all scientists in the TCM (Traditional Chinese Medicine) field." - Tu Youyou*

**Did you know?** Tu Youyou's Nobel Prize in Physiology or Medicine made her the first Chinese citizen to receive a Nobel Prize in the sciences for work carried out within China.

## 10 JUNE

# Rosalía de Castro
Galician Romanticist Poet and Novelist

1837-1885, Spain

A pioneer of modern Galician and Spanish literature, Rosalía's works, rooted in melancholy and nostalgia, highlighted the beauty of the Galician landscape and culture. Her words transcended boundaries, invoking universal feelings of longing and love.

**Did you know?** Both her parents were of noble lineage, but she had a humble upbringing.

## 11 JUNE

# Maria Tallchief
America's Prima Ballerina

1925-2013, USA

Emerging from the Osage Nation in Oklahoma, Maria Tallchief rose to become one of America's premier ballerinas. Her meteoric ascent in the world of ballet began with her training in Los Angeles, leading her to New York City where she shone under George Balanchine's choreography. Tallchief's grace, precision, and passion were unprecedented, making her the first Native American to hold the title of "Prima Ballerina Assoluta." Beyond the limelight, her legacy was cemented as a fierce advocate for arts education and the rights of indigenous people.

> *"Ballet is woman. It is pure. Each gesture is a defining moment."*

**Did you know?** Maria's sister, Marjorie Tallchief, also became a prominent ballerina.

## 12 JUNE
# Rani Lakshmibai
The Warrior Queen of Jhansi

1828-1858, India

A symbol of resistance against British colonization in India, Rani Lakshmibai of Jhansi is celebrated for her bravery during the Indian Rebellion of 1857. Becoming queen at a young age, she trained in sword fighting and horseback riding, embodying both grace and strength. Leading her troops into battle while holding the reins of her young son tied to her back, her fierce spirit remains iconic in Indian history.

*"We fight for independence. In the words of Lord Krishna, we will if we are victorious, enjoy the fruits of victory."*

**Did you know?** Rani Lakshmibai was adept at archery and often practiced with her troops.

## 13 JUNE

# Toni Morrison

Luminous Novelist and Essayist

1931-2019, USA

Toni Morrison's powerful prose illuminated the Black American experience. A Nobel Prize-winning author, she crafted stories that grappled with themes of identity, love, and history. Works like "Beloved" and "Song of Solomon" transcend time, laying bare the wounds of slavery and segregation. Her writing style is distinct, merging the lyricism of oral traditions with a contemporary narrative voice.

*"If there's a book that you want to read, but it hasn't been written yet, then you must write it."*

**Did you know?** Toni Morrison worked as an editor at Random House, amplifying Black voices in literature.

## 14 JUNE

# Hatshepsut

Egypt's Woman Pharaoh

1507-1458 BCE, Egypt

In a world dominated by male rulers, Hatshepsut declared herself Pharaoh, successfully reigning over Egypt during a period of peace and prosperity. She expanded trade routes, commissioned countless architectural projects, and was a major patron of the arts. Her rule was marked by her wisdom and diplomatic acumen, challenging the traditional gender norms of her era.

*"My splendor surpasses that of any king." – from inscriptions at her temple.*

**Did you know?** Hatshepsut had her own obelisks and a remarkable temple at Deir el-Bahri.

## 15 JUNE

# Faye Wattleton

Advocate for Women's Reproductive Rights

1943-Present, USA

Leading the Planned Parenthood Federation of America for over a decade, Faye Wattleton championed women's health and reproductive rights. As the youngest, first woman, and first African American to hold this position, she transformed the organization, establishing it as a political and health care powerhouse.

*"One of the lessons of leadership worth emphasizing is that you want to get to know other great leaders and take their advice."*

**Did you know?** Faye was inducted into the National Women's Hall of Fame in 1993.

## 16 JUNE

# Mae West

Actress and Screenwriter

1893-1980, USA

Mae West, with her inimitable style and daring persona, was a trailblazer in Hollywood. Known for her provocative wit and magnetic screen presence, she not only starred in but also wrote many of her films, challenging the conservative norms and censorship of her era. Her portrayals often celebrated female sexuality and independence, making her a cultural icon and an early feminist symbol in the entertainment industry. Off-screen, her savvy business acumen and advocacy for women's independence marked her as a pioneer in both entertainment and social change.

*"You only live once, but if you do it right, once is enough." - Mae West*

**Did you know?** Before her success in Hollywood, Mae West was a vaudeville sensation, honing her distinct blend of humor and performance that would later define her film career.

## 17 JUNE

# Mary McLeod Bethune
Educator and Civil Rights Activist

1875-1955, USA

Mary McLeod Bethune was a prominent African American educator, stateswoman, philanthropist, humanitarian, and civil rights activist. She is best known for founding the National Council of Negro Women and Bethune-Cookman University. Bethune's lifelong dedication to education and racial equality made her one of the most influential African American women of her time.

*"Invest in the human soul. Who knows, it might be a diamond in the rough."*

**Did you know?** Bethune was an advisor to President Franklin D. Roosevelt, providing insight on minority affairs.

## 18 JUNE
# Kateri Tekakwitha
### The Lily of the Mohawks

1656-1680, New France (now Canada)

Facing tragedy with the loss of her family to smallpox, Kateri, an Algonquin-Mohawk, embraced Christianity. Her devotion led to a life of chastity and acts of penance. Her canonization as a saint in 2012 recognizes her as a symbol of cross-cultural understanding and deep faith.

*"Who will teach me what is most pleasing to God, so that I may do it?"*

**Did you know?** Kateri's face bore smallpox scars, but they miraculously disappeared upon her death.

## 19 JUNE

# Ada Lovelace

The World's First Computer Programmer

1815-1852, England

Ada Lovelace, daughter of the famed poet Lord Byron, defied the norms of her time with her extraordinary mathematical talents. Collaborating with inventor Charles Babbage on the Analytical Engine, a precursor to modern computers, Lovelace wrote what is recognized as the first algorithm intended for machine processing. Her vision for the Analytical Engine's capabilities extended far beyond numerical calculations, anticipating its potential in various fields, essentially predicting the versatility of modern computing.

> *"That brain of mine is something more than merely mortal; as time will show." - Ada Lovelace*

**Did you know?** Ada Lovelace's foresight included the idea that computers could one day create music and art, anticipating the creative and general-purpose use of computing long before it became a reality.

## 20 JUNE
# Betty White
Beloved Actress and Comedian

1922-Present, USA

With a career spanning eight decades, Betty White's enduring humor and charm have captivated audiences globally. From "The Golden Girls" to "Saturday Night Live," her comedic timing and trailblazing roles have earned her a multitude of accolades. Off-screen, her advocacy for animal rights showcases her vast compassion.

*"The older you get, the better you get. Unless you're a banana."*

**Did you know?** Betty holds the Guinness World Record for the longest TV career for a female entertainer.

## 21 JUNE

# Shirley Ann Jackson
Trailblazing Physicist and Educator

1946-Present, USA

Shirley Ann Jackson made history by becoming the first African American woman to earn a Ph.D. from MIT in nuclear physics. Her illustrious career spanned various roles, from research physicist to chairing the U.S. Nuclear Regulatory Commission. Today, she stands as a beacon of academic leadership as the president of Rensselaer Polytechnic Institute.

*"Aim for the high mark and you will hit it. No, not the first time, not the second time and maybe not the third. But keep on aiming and keep on shooting."*

**Did you know?** Jackson was named one of the 50 Most Important Women in Science by Discover Magazine.

## 22 JUNE

# Queen Elizabeth I
England's 'Virgin Queen'

1533-1603, England

The daughter of King Henry VIII and Anne Boleyn, Elizabeth I's reign is termed as the 'Golden Age'. Known for her intellect and strong will, she led England through cultural, economic, and political revivals. During her tenure, the arts flourished, and explorers like Sir Francis Drake circumnavigated the globe.

> *"I know I have the body of a weak, feeble woman; but I have the heart and stomach of a king."*

**Did you know?** Elizabeth I spoke six languages fluently.

## 23 JUNE

# Sonia Sotomayor

Inspirational U.S. Supreme Court Justice

1954-Present, USA

Born to Puerto Rican parents in the Bronx, Sonia Sotomayor's journey from the housing projects to the highest court is nothing short of remarkable. As the first Hispanic and third woman appointed to the U.S. Supreme Court, her rulings emphasize justice, human rights, and equality.

*"Don't mistake politeness for lack of strength."*

**Did you know?** Sotomayor saved Major League Baseball from a strike in 1995 with her ruling.

## 24 JUNE

# Miriam Makeba
### The Voice of Africa

1932-2008, South Africa

Miriam Makeba, affectionately known as 'Mama Africa', used her vocal talents to spotlight the brutalities of apartheid. Exiled for her activism, she performed globally, introducing many to African rhythms while advocating for freedom and equality in her homeland.

*"Age is...wisdom, if one has lived one's life properly."*

**Did you know?** Makeba was the first African artist to popularize African music in the U.S. in the 1960s.

## 25 JUNE

# Maria Callas
Opera's Divine Diva

1923-1977, USA and Greece

Maria Callas, with her transformative performances and dramatic intensity, was one of the 20th century's foremost sopranos. Her life was filled with passion, not just on stage but off, with tumultuous love affairs and fierce media scrutiny.

*"When music fails to agree to the ear, to soothe the ear and the heart and the senses, then it has missed the point."*

**Did you know?** Callas had a dramatic weight loss, which some believe affected her vocal cords.

## 26 JUNE

# Golda Meir

Israel's Iron-willed Prime Minister

1898-1978, Ukraine to USA to Israel

From Milwaukee schoolteacher to Israel's prime minister, Golda Meir's dedication to the Jewish state was unwavering. In the tumultuous realm of Middle Eastern politics, her leadership during critical moments, like the Yom Kippur War, proved pivotal.

*"Trust yourself. Create the kind of self that you will be happy to live with all your life."*

**Did you know?** Golda worked as a kibbutz farmer in her early years in Palestine.

## 27 JUNE

# Wang Zhenyi

China's Astronomical Genius

1768-1797, China

In an era when women's educational pursuits were limited, Wang Zhenyi self-taught herself astronomy, mathematics, and poetry. Her works demystified complex celestial concepts, and her innovative experiments, like the lunar eclipse demonstration, were groundbreaking.

> *"It's made to believe, Women are the same as Men; Are you not convinced, Daughters can also be heroic?"*

**Did you know?** Wang defied societal norms of her time by dressing as a man to attend public events.

## 28 JUNE
# Temple Grandin
Advocate for Autism and Animal Behavior

1947-Present, USA

Temple Grandin, diagnosed with autism as a child, became a leading voice in both autism advocacy and animal behavior. Her innovative designs for livestock-handling facilities showcased her unique visual thinking, and her insights on autism have shaped global understanding.

*"Nature is cruel, but we don't have to be."*

**Did you know?** Grandin invented the "hug machine" to calm hypersensitive people.

## 29 JUNE

# Florence Nightingale
### The Lady with the Lamp

1820-1910, England

Regarded as the founder of modern nursing, Florence Nightingale's tireless work during the Crimean War reformed healthcare. Beyond her hands-on care, her statistical work laid foundations for evidence-based medicine. Her night rounds, lamp in hand, earned her an enduring nickname.

*"I attribute my success to this - I never gave or took any excuse."*

**Did you know?** Nightingale was a prolific writer and penned around 200 books, reports, and pamphlets.

## 30 JUNE
# Christine de Pizan
Medieval Feminist and Author

1364-c.1430, Italy to France

Christine de Pizan was a pioneering figure in feminist literature. Born in Italy and later moving to France, she emerged as a powerful voice against the prevailing gender biases of her time. Her most famous work, "The Book of the City of Ladies," is a compelling defense of women, drawing upon historical and mythical figures to counteract the pervasive misogyny in medieval society. Through her eloquent writings, Christine advocated for women's intellectual capacity and moral strength, challenging the subservient roles typically assigned to them.

*"Just as women's bodies are softer than men's, so their understanding is sharper."*

**Did you know?** Christine de Pizan's success as a professional writer was highly unusual for a woman of her time, making her a trailblazer for female authors in an era when women's contributions to literature were often dismissed or overlooked.

# JULY

## 1 JULY

# Princess Pingyang

The Warrior Princess of the Tang Dynasty

598-623, China

When rebellion struck the Tang Dynasty, Princess Pingyang didn't recline in her royal chambers. She formed an all-women "Army of the Lady" and played a crucial role in her father's rise to the throne. Pingyang showed that princesses could be fierce warriors and strategic thinkers, shattering the mold of typical royal expectations.

*"In the face of injustice, even a princess must take up arms."*

**Did you know?** Princess Pingyang's legacy was so revered that despite traditions, her father gave her a full military funeral when she passed away.

## 2 JULY
# Greta Thunberg
Climate Change Activist Extraordinaire

2003-Present, Sweden

With a sign reading "Skolstrejk för klimatet" (School strike for climate), Greta began a global movement. By skipping school to sit outside the Swedish parliament, she ignited a worldwide youth movement for climate change, reminding everyone, young and old, of our responsibility to our planet.

*"Our house is on fire."*

**Did you know?** Greta's activism began at age 15 and has since sparked millions to join the Fridays for Future movement.

## 3 JULY

# Ruth Bader Ginsburg

U.S. Supreme Court Justice &
Gender Equality Advocate

1933-2020, USA

Ruth Bader Ginsburg, affectionately known as "RBG", was a trailblazer for gender equality. As a lawyer, she won multiple landmark cases against gender discrimination. Later, as a Supreme Court Justice, she continued to champion women's rights, leaving an indelible mark on American jurisprudence.

*"Fight for the things that you care about, but do it in a way that will lead others to join you."*

**Did you know?** RBG was one of only nine women in her Harvard Law School class of 500 students.

4 JULY

# Queen Tamar of Georgia
Georgia's Most Celebrated Monarch

1160-1213, Georgia

Queen Tamar of Georgia reigned during the nation's Golden Age and was far more than a symbolic monarch. Her rule was characterized by significant territorial expansion, cultural flourishing, and diplomatic success. Tamar's reign was marked by a strong central government, military victories, and the promotion of Georgian Orthodox Christianity. She fostered an environment where arts and literature thrived, commissioning works and buildings that remain historical treasures. Her leadership demonstrated that a woman could rule with the wisdom, strength, and vision traditionally ascribed to kings.

*"A land led by a woman is a land like no other"*

**Did you know?** Under Queen Tamar's reign, the Georgian Kingdom reached its greatest extent, controlling territories far beyond its traditional borders and becoming a dominant regional power.

## 5 JULY

# Mary Cassatt

Pioneering Impressionist Painter

1844-1926, USA/France

Mary Cassatt's exquisite paintings of domestic life and mother-child bonds made her one of the leading artists of the Impressionist movement. Though American-born, she spent most of her life in France, breaking barriers in the male-dominated art world of the time.

*"Art is not subject to politics...Art has its universality."*

**Did you know?** Many of her paintings were inspired by her close relationship with her sister Lydia.

## 6 JULY
# Gertrude Stein
Literary Innovator and Art Collector

1874-1946, USA/France

Gertrude Stein was more than just a writer; she was a catalyst for change. Residing in Paris, her home became a hub for budding artists and writers. Stein's distinct writing style, playing with repetition and rhythm, influenced many 20th-century authors.

*"A rose is a rose is a rose."*

**Did you know?** Gertrude Stein and her partner, Alice B. Toklas, collected works of artists like Picasso and Matisse before they were globally renowned.

## 7 JULY

# Viola Liuzzo

Civil Rights Activist and Martyr

1925-1965, USA

From Michigan to Alabama, Viola Liuzzo's commitment to civil rights knew no bounds. A mother of five, she was deeply moved by the injustices against African Americans and joined the Selma marches. Sadly, she was murdered by Ku Klux Klan members, but her legacy of courage and conviction lives on.

*"If I died, I died for freedom."*

**Did you know?** Viola was the only known white female killed during the Civil Rights Movement.

## 8 JULY

# Annie Oakley

Sharpshooter and Western Star

1860-1926, USA

From humble beginnings, Annie Oakley rose to become one of America's first female superstars. Her impeccable marksmanship skills led her to star in Buffalo Bill's Wild West show, defying traditional gender roles and proving women could shoot just as well, if not better, than men.

*"Aim at a high mark and you'll hit it."*

**Did you know?** Annie Oakley could split a playing card edge-on and put five or six more holes in it before it touched the ground.

## 9 JULY

# Eleanor Roosevelt

First Lady and Human Rights Champion

1884-1962, USA

Eleanor Roosevelt redefined the role of the First Lady, advocating for human rights, women's rights, and children's causes. After her time in the White House, she played a pivotal role in drafting the Universal Declaration of Human Rights, proving her dedication to global betterment.

*"The future belongs to those who believe in the beauty of their dreams."*

**Did you know?** Eleanor wrote a six-day-a-week newspaper column called "My Day," discussing social and political issues.

## 10 JULY
# Lorraine Hansberry
Playwright of "A Raisin in the Sun"

1930-1965, USA

Lorraine Hansberry's groundbreaking play, "A Raisin in the Sun," illuminated the struggles and aspirations of an African American family in the 1950s. As the first Black woman to have a play performed on Broadway, Hansberry's work paved the way for future Black playwrights.

> *"The thing that makes you exceptional, if you are at all, is inevitably that which must also make you lonely."*

**Did you know?** Lorraine was involved in civil rights activism, attending a peace conference that led her to being under FBI surveillance.

## 11 JULY

# Soraya Tarzi
### The Modern Queen of Afghanistan

1899-1968, Afghanistan

Queen Soraya Tarzi, a visionary figure in Afghan history, was dedicated to modernizing Afghanistan during her tenure as queen consort. She was a champion of women's rights, advocating for education and social freedoms. Working alongside King Amanullah Khan, Soraya played a crucial role in promoting reforms aimed at transforming Afghanistan into a more progressive and modern society. Her efforts in advancing women's causes marked a significant chapter in the country's history.

> *"There is no value in the universe over a woman's innocence."*

**Did you know?** Queen Soraya was a symbol of modernity and change in Afghanistan, and her image on the Afghan banknote was a testament to her influence and legacy.

## 12 JULY
# Esther Afua Ocloo
Ghanaian Entrepreneur and Microlending Pioneer

1919-2002, Ghana

Esther Afua Ocloo began her entrepreneurial journey with as little as sixpence, given to her by an aunt. She used it to buy oranges, which she made into marmalade and sold. Esther was not only innovative but also possessed a keen business acumen. Eventually, her endeavors expanded into what we now know as the Nkulenu Industries, one of Ghana's most prosperous food-processing businesses.

*"You are not complete no matter how much money you have until you help your people."*

**Did you know?** Esther was one of the founders of Women's World Banking, a global nonprofit aimed at giving low-income women access to financial tools.

## 13 JULY

# Gabriela Mistral

Nobel Prize-Winning Chilean Poet

1889-1957, Chile

Gabriela Mistral was a pivotal figure in Latin American literature. She was the first Latin American woman to win the Nobel Prize for Literature, earned through her deep and soulful poems. Her works were woven with themes of love, sorrow, and social justice, and they continue to be studied and cherished today.

*"At this point, I can't do more than love you, and leave you the inheritance of my sadness."*

**Did you know?** Gabriela Mistral was not her real name. She chose the pen name by combining two of her favorite poets, Gabriele D'Annunzio and Frédéric Mistral.

## 14 JULY
# Annie Besant
Social Reformer and Theosophist

1847-1933, United Kingdom/India

Annie Besant was a woman of many talents: a social reformer, an advocate for Indian independence, and a leading figure in the Theosophical Society. Originally from London, she was drawn to India by her quest for spiritual understanding and quickly immersed herself in Indian culture and politics.

*"Better remain silent, better not even think, if you are not prepared to act."*

**Did you know?** Annie Besant was the first woman to become the president of the Indian National Congress.

## 15 JULY

# Angela Davis

Political Activist and Scholar

can 1944-Present, USA

Angela Davis is a towering figure in the fight against social injustice in America. From her early days as a philosophy professor to her activism and political candidacy, Davis has been a relentless advocate for civil rights, particularly in relation to race, gender, and prison reform.

*"I am no longer accepting the things I cannot change. I am changing the things I cannot accept."*

**Did you know?** Angela Davis was once on the FBI's Most Wanted list due to her activism but was acquitted of all charges.

## 16 JULY

# Anna Julia Cooper
Black Feminist Scholar and Educator

1858-1964, USA

Anna Julia Cooper stands out as one of the most important black scholars in American history. Born into slavery, she later became the fourth African-American woman to earn a Ph.D. Her book, "A Voice from the South," is considered an early text in black feminism.

*"The cause of freedom is not the cause of a race or a sect, a party or a class—it is the cause of humankind, the very birthright of humanity."*

**Did you know?** Anna Julia Cooper lived to be 105 and saw the Civil Rights Movement take shape.

## 17 JULY

# Anna May Wong

Hollywood's First Chinese American Star

1905-1961, USA

Anna May Wong broke barriers in a Hollywood that was often unwelcoming to non-white actors. Born in Los Angeles to second-generation Chinese-Americans, Wong began her film career during the silent film era. As she navigated typecasting and discriminatory practices, Wong used her platform to challenge Hollywood's narrow portrayal of Asian characters. Her talent shone in films like "The Toll of the Sea" and "Shanghai Express."

> *"I was so tired of the parts I had to play. There seems little for me in Hollywood, because, rather than real Chinese, producers prefer Hungarians, Mexicans, American Indians for Chinese roles."*

**Did you know?** Anna May Wong was fluent in several languages, including German and French, and she enjoyed success in European films.

*365 INSPIRING WOMEN*

## 18 JULY
# Margaret Bourke-White
Groundbreaking Photojournalist

1904-1971, USA

A pioneer in her field, Margaret Bourke-White was the first American female war photojournalist. With her fearless spirit, she captured powerful images from the Dust Bowl, the liberation of Buchenwald, and Gandhi's last hours. Her photos for LIFE magazine showcased her unique ability to be at the right place at the right time.

*"The camera is a remarkable instrument. Saturate yourself with your subject, and the camera will all but take you by the hand and point the way."*

**Did you know?** Margaret Bourke-White was the first female photographer to be allowed in combat zones during World War II.

## 19 JULY

# Eva Perón

Argentina's Spiritual Leader of the Nation

1919-1952, Argentina

Eva Perón, often called "Evita," captured Argentina's heart with her charisma and dedication to the working class. Beginning life in rural Argentina, she climbed the social ladder using her talents in acting. As the First Lady, she championed labor rights, women's suffrage, and the well-being of the poor, leaving a lasting legacy.

*"I will return and be millions."*

**Did you know?** Evita's legacy continues to influence Argentine politics, with many political parties using her image in campaigns.

## 20 JULY

# Simone Biles
Gymnastics Phenomenon

1997-Present, USA

A gymnast with unparalleled skill, Simone Biles has been recognized as one of the greatest of all time. With numerous Olympic and World Championship medals, Biles continues to push the boundaries of her sport. Off the mat, she advocates for athletes' mental health and stands against abuse within sports.

*"Sometimes I wish I could have an out-of-body experience to witness it, because sometimes I think I'm going crazy."*

**Did you know?** Simone has multiple gymnastic moves named after her because she was the first to perform them in major competitions.

## 21 JULY

# Cornelia Africana
Defender of Roman Virtues

190-100 BCE, Ancient Rome

As the daughter of Scipio Africanus, Cornelia Africana was a prominent figure in ancient Rome. Beyond her family ties, she was revered for her wisdom, virtue, and commitment to education. Cornelia raised two of Rome's influential reformers, Tiberius and Gaius Gracchus, and became an emblem of the ideal Roman matron.

*"If I am to point to the jewels of my house, I point to my sons."*

**Did you know?** There are statues and coins made in Cornelia's likeness, a rare honor for women in ancient Rome.

## 22 JULY

# Queen Moremi of Ile-Ife
### The Brave Yoruba Heroine

12th century, Ile-Ife (present-day Nigeria)

Queen Moremi of Ile-Ife is a legendary figure in Yoruba history, celebrated for her extraordinary bravery and self-sacrifice. When her kingdom faced frequent raids, Moremi risked her life by infiltrating the enemy's camp to uncover their vulnerabilities. Her successful espionage led to the liberation of her people, but it came at a personal cost. Her story is a powerful testament to the courage and resilience of women in leadership.

*"True bravery is doing what is right, even when it's against one's personal interest."*

**Did you know?** The Edi festival in Ile-Ife is a vibrant celebration commemorating Moremi's sacrifice and valor, illustrating the lasting impact of her heroic deeds.

## 23 JULY

# Vandana Shiva

Environmental Activist and Author

1952-Present, India

Vandana Shiva has been at the forefront of the global eco-feminist movement, championing biodiversity, organic farming, and rights of farmers. She has fiercely critiqued corporate-led agriculture and its impact on small-scale farmers. Her books and teachings emphasize sustainable agriculture and grassroots activism.

*"We are either going to have a future where women lead the way to make peace with the Earth, or we are not going to have a human future at all."*

**Did you know?** Vandana Shiva started the Navdanya movement, which has helped thousands of Indian farmers practice sustainable farming.

## 24 JULY

# Malala Yousafzai
Advocate for Girls' Education

1997-Present, Pakistan

Shot by the Taliban for attending school, Malala Yousafzai's survival and subsequent activism made her an international symbol for girls' education. Despite the attempt on her life, Malala remains undeterred and continues her advocacy, emphasizing the importance of education for all. In 2014, she became the youngest recipient of the Nobel Peace Prize.

*"One child, one teacher, one book, and one pen can change the world."*

**Did you know?** Malala started her activism by writing a blog for BBC Urdu detailing life under the Taliban.

## 25 JULY

# Olive Yang

Myanmar's Rebel Princess

1927-2017, Myanmar (Burma)

From royalty to opium warlord to peacemaker, Olive Yang's life was anything but ordinary. Defying traditional norms, she donned men's attire and led her own militia in Myanmar's lawless Shan State. Though initially involved in opium trade, she later collaborated with government forces to stem the flow of narcotics.

*"In a world that demands conformity, dare to be the anomaly."*

**Did you know?** Olive Yang was a close confidante of the Dalai Lama during his 1959 escape to India.

## 26 JULY
# Cai Wenji
Renowned Poet and Musician of Ancient China

177-250, China

Kidnapped and taken far from her home during a tumultuous period in China, Cai Wenji spent twelve years among the Xiongnu nomads. Despite her hardship, she composed music and poetry reflecting her experiences. Upon her eventual return, she became a symbol of cultural resilience.

*"Though the world changes, the heart's tune remains the same."*

**Did you know?** Cai Wenji's compositions serve as important records of events and feelings of her era.

## 27 JULY

# Fanny Mendelssohn
Composer Overshadowed by a Brother

1805-1847, Germany

While her brother Felix is well-known, Fanny Mendelssohn was an equally talented musician. However, societal norms restricted her from publicly showcasing her work. Nevertheless, she composed over 460 pieces of music, showcasing her depth and genius.

*"Music is my language, the expression of my innermost self."*

**Did you know?** Fanny's compositions were sometimes published under her brother's name due to societal prejudices against female composers.

## 28 JULY
# Maryam Mirzakhani
### First Female Fields Medalist

1977-2017, Iran/USA

Breaking gender barriers in mathematics, Maryam Mirzakhani became the first woman to win the Fields Medal, often regarded as the "Nobel Prize of Mathematics." Her work in geometry and dynamics has left an indelible mark on the world of mathematics.

*"You have to spend some energy and effort to see the beauty of math."*

**Did you know?** Maryam often sketched her mathematical proofs, turning complex ideas into intricate drawings.

## 29 JULY

# Fannie Farmer

Culinary Expert and Cookbook Author

1857-1915, USA

Fannie Farmer was an American culinary expert whose cookbook "The Boston Cooking-School Cook Book" revolutionized American cooking through the introduction of standardized measurements. She is also known for her lectures on diet and nutrition, emphasizing the importance of proper meal planning for the sick and convalescent.

> *"Progress in civilization has been accompanied by progress in cookery."*

**Did you know?** Farmer opened Miss Farmer's School of Cookery in Boston, aiming to train housewives and nurses in dietetics and cookery.

## 30 JULY

# Wangari Maathai

Environmentalist and Nobel Laureate

1940-2011, Kenya

Founder of the Green Belt Movement, Wangari Maathai worked tirelessly to promote environmental conservation in Kenya. She empowered women to plant trees, combatting deforestation and providing them with a livelihood. In 2004, she became the first African woman to receive the Nobel Peace Prize.

*"Until you dig a hole, you plant a tree, you water it and make it survive, you haven't done a thing. You are just talking."*

**Did you know?** Wangari Maathai was the first woman in East and Central Africa to earn a doctorate degree.

## 31 JULY

# Artemisia Gentileschi
Pioneering Female Baroque Artist

1593-1656, Italy

Artemisia Gentileschi, a trailblazing female artist of the Baroque era, overcame personal trauma and societal barriers to achieve fame. Her works, characterized by dramatic intensity and a unique perspective on female subjects, challenged the norms of her time. Gentileschi's "Judith Slaying Holofernes" is not only a visual masterpiece but also a statement on female power and resilience, reflecting her own experiences with the legal and social challenges of her era. *"I will show Your Illustrious Lordship what a woman can do."*
**Did you know?** Artemisia Gentileschi's legacy extends beyond her art; she is celebrated as a pioneering figure for women in the arts, inspiring generations of female artists to pursue their passions in the face of adversity.

365 INSPIRING WOMEN

# AUGUST

## 1 AUGUST
# Gloria E. Anzaldúa
Scholar, Cultural Theorist, and Feminist Icon

1942-2004, USA

Gloria E. Anzaldúa's writings weave a powerful narrative of life on the U.S.-Mexico border, exploring themes of race, identity, and post-colonialism. Her seminal work, "Borderlands/La Frontera," redefined feminist, queer, and Chicana thought, highlighting the challenges and unique experiences of women living in the borderlands.

> *"To survive the Borderlands, you must live sin fronteras [sin], be a crossroads."*

**Did you know?** Anzaldúa was openly lesbian and integrated her experiences into her exploration of Chicana feminist theory.

## 2 AUGUST

# Empress Ma
Tang Dynasty Matriarch

40-79, China

Empress Ma, a respected figure in the early Han dynasty, exercised significant influence during her husband Emperor Guangwu's reign. Beyond her political acumen, Empress Ma was known for her virtue, diligence, and generosity, becoming a revered role model in Chinese imperial history.

*"Behind the throne's power, stands the wisdom of a woman."*

**Did you know?** Despite being an empress, Ma always exhibited humility and wore simple clothes even during ceremonial occasions.

## 3 AUGUST

# Sor Juana Inez de la Cruz
### The Tenth Muse of Mexico

1648–1695, Mexico

A self-taught scholar and poet of the Baroque school, Sor Juana was a nun who dedicated her life to studying and writing. Facing criticism for her opinions and works, she penned "Respuesta a Sor Filotea," defending women's right to knowledge and education.

> *"One can perfectly well philosophize while cooking supper."*

**Did you know?** Sor Juana amassed one of the largest private libraries in the Americas, but had to sell all her books due to pressure from the church.

## 4 AUGUST
# Nancy Pelosi
Groundbreaking US Politician

1940-Present, USA

As the first and only woman to serve as Speaker of the U.S. House of Representatives, Nancy Pelosi shattered political glass ceilings. A fierce advocate for healthcare, environment, and human rights, Pelosi has navigated the intricacies of Washington with determination and tact.

*"Know your power. Every one of us has something to give."*

**Did you know?** Pelosi was involved in politics from a young age; her father was a Congressman and Mayor of Baltimore.

## 5 AUGUST

# Maria Mitchell

America's First Female Astronomer

1818-1889, USA

Discovering a new comet at age 29, Maria Mitchell's achievement earned her global recognition. Advocating for women in science, she became the first female astronomy professor in the U.S. and inspired countless women to pursue careers in STEM.

> *"We especially need imagination in science. It is not all mathematics, nor all logic, but it is somewhat beauty and poetry."*

**Did you know?** In recognition of her contributions, a World War II Liberty Ship was named after Maria Mitchell.

## 6 AUGUST

# Queen Seondeok of Silla

Korea's Visionary Monarch

606-647, Korea

The first female ruler of the Korean kingdom of Silla, Queen Seondeok's reign was marked by cultural prosperity and political stability. A lover of arts and sciences, she fostered relationships with scholars and promoted Buddhism as the state religion.

*"A wise ruler listens, learns, and leads."*

**Did you know?** The star-gazing tower, Cheomseongdae, built during her reign, is one of the oldest surviving observatories in East Asia.

## 7 AUGUST

# Leila Aboulela
Celebrated Sudanese Writer

1964-Present, Sudan/UK

Leila Aboulela's novels and stories beautifully capture the intricacies of Islamic spirituality and the immigrant experience. Her works, including "Minaret" and "The Translator," are celebrated for their poetic prose and deep introspection.

*"Stories can be lighthouses. They throw light on our own dilemmas, fears, and desires."*

**Did you know?** Aboulela's writings have been recognized for bridging cultural gaps, and she has won numerous awards, including the Caine Prize for African Writing.

## 8 AUGUST

# Sally Ride

First American Woman in Space

1951-2012, USA

Shattering the space ceiling, Sally Ride became the first American woman astronaut to travel to space. Her journey on the Challenger space shuttle was more than just a mission; it symbolized possibilities for young girls everywhere.

*"You can't be what you can't see."*

**Did you know?** Sally Ride used her platform to advocate for science education, especially for girls, establishing Sally Ride Science, an educational company.

## 9 AUGUST

# Queen Mavia

Fierce Warrior Queen of the Tanukhids

4th century, Near East

Leading her nomadic tribe against the mighty Roman Empire, Queen Mavia's military strategy and tactics earned her respect even from her enemies. Negotiating a peace treaty on her terms, she emerged as one of the most influential leaders of her time.

*"The strength of a leader is reflected in the resilience of her people."*

**Did you know?** Historical accounts often liken Mavia's leadership skills and military tactics to those of the legendary Queen Zenobia of Palmyra.

## 10 AUGUST

# Taylor Swift

Global Pop Icon and Advocate

1989-Present, USA

From country darling to international pop sensation, Taylor Swift's music career is marked by chart-topping albums and heartfelt songwriting. Beyond her musical prowess, Swift actively advocates for artists' rights and has spoken out on political and social issues.

*"I want to be defined by the things that I love. Not the things I'm afraid of, or the things that haunt me in the middle of the night."*

**Did you know?** Swift was the youngest recipient ever of the Grammy Award for Album of the Year at age 20.

## 11 AUGUST

# Emma Watson

Actress and Activist

1990-Present, UK

Best known for her role as Hermione Granger in the "Harry Potter" series, Emma Watson has used her global platform to advocate for gender equality. As a UN Women Goodwill Ambassador, she launched the "HeForShe" campaign to promote gender solidarity.

*"If not me, who? If not now, when?"*

**Did you know?** Emma Watson graduated from Brown University with a bachelor's degree in English literature.

## 12 AUGUST

# Zora Neale Hurston

Renowned African-American Author and Anthropologist

1891-1960, USA

Zora Neale Hurston was a key figure of the Harlem Renaissance, a literary and artistic movement celebrating black life and culture. She authored several novels, short stories, and plays, but her most famous work is "Their Eyes Were Watching God." Hurston's writings focused on African-American experiences and folklore, often examining gender roles and racial struggles.

*"There are years that ask questions and years that answer."*

**Did you know?** Hurston also conducted anthropological research, collecting African-American folk tales in the rural South.

## 13 AUGUST

# Sacagawea

### Guide and Interpreter of the Lewis and Clark Expedition

c. 1788-1812, USA

Sacagawea, a Lemhi Shoshone woman, played an indispensable role in the Lewis and Clark Expedition as a guide and interpreter. Her knowledge of the geography and her diplomatic presence were invaluable in the successful navigation and negotiations with various Native American tribes.

*"I am not afraid to go."*

**Did you know?** Sacagawea carried her infant son, Jean Baptiste, on her back throughout the expedition.

## 14 AUGUST

# Betty Friedan

Catalyst of the Second-Wave Feminist Movement

1921-2006, USA

Author of "The Feminine Mystique," Betty Friedan challenged the prevailing mid-20th-century notion of women's fulfillment in housework and motherhood. Her book is often credited with sparking the second wave of American feminism. Friedan also co-founded the National Organization for Women (NOW), playing a pivotal role in advocating for women's rights.

*"The problem that has no name — which is simply the fact that American women are kept from growing to their full human capacities — is taking a far greater toll on the physical and mental health of our country than any known disease."*

**Did you know?** Friedan organized the Women's Strike for Equality in 1970, one of the largest feminist protests in American history.

## 15 AUGUST

# Nefertiti

Iconic Queen of Ancient Egypt

c. 1370-1330 BCE, Egypt

Nefertiti, whose name means "a beautiful woman has come," was the queen of Egypt and wife of Pharaoh Akhenaten. She is known for her elegance and is often depicted in art and sculptures. Nefertiti may have ruled as Pharaoh herself after her husband's death, a rare occurrence in ancient Egypt.

*"Beauty is the radiance of truth, and the frill on the hem of a garment of delight."*

**Did you know?** The famous bust of Nefertiti, discovered in 1912, is one of the most copied works of ancient Egypt.

## 16 AUGUST

# Toni Stone

Boundary-Breaking Baseball Player

1921-1996, USA

As the first of three women to play professional baseball in the Negro Leagues, Toni Stone broke significant gender barriers. Playing amidst racism and sexism, Stone held her own against male counterparts, showing exceptional skill and resilience on the field.

*"They say I'm the best woman player in baseball. I say I'm the best player, period."*

**Did you know?** Stone hit a single off the legendary Satchel Paige, one of her proudest moments.

## 17 AUGUST

# Amelia Earhart

Pioneering Aviator

1897-1939, USA

Amelia Earhart, the first woman to fly solo across the Atlantic Ocean, became an icon of courage and determination. Her numerous aviation records and her mysterious disappearance during a circumnavigational flight attempt have made her a legendary figure in the history of flight.

*"The most effective way to do it, is to do it."*

**Did you know?** Earhart was also an author and wrote several best-selling books about her flying experiences.

## 18 AUGUST
# Sojourner Truth
Abolitionist and Women's Rights Activist

c. 1797-1883, USA

Born into slavery, Sojourner Truth escaped with her infant daughter and became a prominent abolitionist and women's rights activist. Her famous speech, "Ain't I a Woman," delivered at the Ohio Women's Rights Convention in 1851, is known for its powerful and poignant call for equal rights.

*"I feel safe in the midst of my enemies, for the truth is all powerful and will prevail."*

**Did you know?** Sojourner Truth couldn't read or write, but her speeches, dictated to others, were widely published.

## 19 AUGUST

# Olive Morris

British Activist for Racial and Gender Equality

1952-1979, UK

Olive Morris was a fearless activist who campaigned for racial, gender, and social equality in Britain. A founding member of several influential groups, she fought against police brutality, housing inequality, and discrimination.

> *"The struggle is a never-ending process. Freedom is never really won. You earn it and win it in every generation."*

**Did you know?** Despite her short life, Olive's impact was profound, and a community building in Brixton was named in her honor.

## 20 AUGUST

# Queen Maya

Mother of the Buddha

c. 5th century BCE, Ancient Nepal

Queen Maya of Sakya was the mother of Siddhartha Gautama, who later became known as the Buddha. Her story is one of reverence in Buddhist traditions. She is often depicted in art and literature and is remembered for her purity and grace.

*"A mother's love illuminates the path to enlightenment."*

**Did you know?** In Buddhist art, Queen Maya is often depicted holding onto a tree branch, symbolizing the naturalness and ease of her son's birth.

## 21 AUGUST

# Julia Child

Renowned American Chef and TV Personality

1912-2004, USA

Julia Child transformed American cooking through her cookbook, "Mastering the Art of French Cooking," and her television show, "The French Chef." Known for her exuberant personality and encouraging approach, she demystified French cuisine, making it accessible to mainstream America.

*"The only real stumbling block is fear of failure. In cooking, you've got to have a what-the-hell attitude."*

**Did you know?** Julia Child was a secret intelligence officer before she became a famous chef.

## 22 AUGUST

# Teresa de Cofrentes
Medieval Mystic and Visionary

15th Century, Spain

Teresa de Cofrentes, a figure shrouded in history, was a Spanish mystic known for her profound spiritual visions. Living during a time when women's voices were seldom heard, especially in religious contexts, Teresa's writings and teachings were daring and revolutionary.

*"In the depth of silence, one hears the truth."*

**Did you know?** Teresa's visions and teachings were carefully documented by her followers, preserving her legacy.

## 23 AUGUST

# Patti Smith
Punk Rock Poet Laureate

1946-Present, USA

Dubbed the "punk poet laureate," Patti Smith's fusion of rock and poetry reshaped the American music landscape. Her 1975 album "Horses" is a landmark in the history of rock music, blending raw, honest lyrics with powerful melodies.

*"People have the power to redeem the work of fools."*

**Did you know?** Patti Smith is also an accomplished author, with her memoir "Just Kids" winning the National Book Award.

## 24 AUGUST
# Elizabeth Cady Stanton
## Women's Rights Pioneer

1815-1902, USA

A leading figure of the early women's rights movement in the United States, Elizabeth Cady Stanton was instrumental in initiating the first women's suffrage movement in the U.S. Her Declaration of Sentiments, presented at the Seneca Falls Convention in 1848, is a landmark document in the history of women's rights in America.

*"The best protection any woman can have... is courage."*

**Did you know?** Stanton often collaborated with Susan B. Anthony, another key figure in the suffrage movement.

## 25 AUGUST

# Marianne North
Pioneering Botanical Artist

1830-1890, United Kingdom

Marianne North was an English Victorian biologist and botanical artist known for her detailed plant and landscape paintings from her extensive travels. She broke the conventions of the time, traveling alone to remote locations. Her collection is displayed in the Marianne North Gallery at the Royal Botanic Gardens, Kew.

*"I had long dreamed of going to some tropical country to paint its peculiar vegetation on the spot in natural abundant luxuriance."*

**Did you know?** North painted over 800 species of plants, many of which were unknown to science at the time.

## 26 AUGUST

# Ella Baker

Civil Rights and Human Rights Activist

1903-1986, USA

A lesser-known but immensely influential figure in the civil rights movement, Ella Baker worked behind the scenes, empowering grassroots leaders. She believed in collective leadership and was instrumental in the formation of the Student Nonviolent Coordinating Committee (SNCC).

*"Strong people don't need strong leaders."*

**Did you know?** Baker criticized the top-down leadership approach of some male-dominated civil rights organizations.

## 27 AUGUST

# Isabel Allende

Celebrated Latin American Author

1942-Present, Peru/Chile

Isabel Allende, a renowned novelist, weaves tales rich with elements of magic realism and strong female characters. Her novels, such as "The House of the Spirits" and "City of the Beasts," often draw from her personal experiences and Chilean cultural history.

*"Write what should not be forgotten."*

**Did you know?** Allende started writing on January 8, and now considers it her lucky day to start new books.

## 28 AUGUST
# Amelia Boynton Robinson
Civil Rights Pioneer

1911-2015, USA

A key figure in the Selma Voting Rights Movement and the first African-American woman in Alabama to run for Congress, Amelia Boynton Robinson was a trailblazer for civil rights and voting rights. She was instrumental in organizing the Selma to Montgomery marches in 1965.

*"Be certain that you do not die without having done something wonderful for humanity."*

**Did you know?** Amelia was brutally beaten during the "Bloody Sunday" march but remained a staunch activist throughout her life.

## 29 AUGUST

# Dorothy Height

Unsung Heroine of the Civil Rights Movement

1912-2010, USA

Often called the "godmother of the civil rights movement," Dorothy Height dedicated her life to fighting for African-American rights and women's rights. She led the National Council of Negro Women for four decades and was a key organizer of the famous 1963 March on Washington.

*"If the time is not ripe, we have to ripen the time."*

**Did you know?** Height was awarded the Presidential Medal of Freedom in 1994.

## 30 AUGUST

# Hedy Lamarr

Actress and Inventor

1914-2000, Austria/USA

Hedy Lamarr was not just a renowned actress; she was also an inventor. Her most significant contribution was co-inventing a radio guidance system during World War II, which later became a cornerstone for modern wireless communication technologies like Bluetooth and Wi-Fi.

*"All creative people want to do the unexpected."*

**Did you know?** Lamarr's invention was initially dismissed and not implemented until later.

## 31 AUGUST

# Berta Cáceres

Environmental Activist and Indigenous Leader

1971-2016, Honduras

Berta Cáceres was a courageous environmental activist and indigenous leader. She co-founded the Council of Popular and Indigenous Organizations of Honduras (COPINH) and was a staunch defender of the Lenca people's land and rights, opposing mega-projects like the Agua Zarca Dam.

*"Let us wake up! We're out of time. We must shake our conscience free of the rapacious capitalism, racism, and patriarchy that will only assure our own self-destruction."*

**Did you know?** Berta Cáceres won the prestigious Goldman Environmental Prize in 2015.

365 INSPIRING WOMEN

# SEPTEMBER

## 1 SEPTEMBER

# Hildegard of Bingen

Visionary Abbess and Polymath

1098-1179, Germany

Hildegard of Bingen, a Benedictine abbess, was a writer, composer, philosopher, Christian mystic, and visionary. She was a pioneer in several fields, from theology to natural history. Hildegard's compositions and writings, including "Scivias" and "Ordo Virtutum," are celebrated for their creativity and depth. She is also known for her profound spiritual visions which were influential in religious circles of the time.

*"The earth is at the same time mother, she is mother of all that is natural, mother of all that is human..."*

**Did you know?** Hildegard was considered a founder of scientific natural history in Germany.

## 2 SEPTEMBER

# Ban Zhao

China's First Female Historian

c. 35-100, China

Ban Zhao, the first known female Chinese historian, completed her brother Ban Gu's work on the "Book of Han," a critical history of the Western Han dynasty. She was also an esteemed poet and essayist, writing works such as "Lessons for Women," which outlined the conduct expected of women in her time.

*"To be a woman is to have interest in family affairs and a lack of selfish desires."*

**Did you know?** Ban Zhao was also a teacher and advisor at the imperial court.

## 3 SEPTEMBER

# Queen Ranavalona I of Madagascar

### The Merina Monarch

c. 1788-1861, Madagascar

Queen Ranavalona I, also known as Ranavalona the Cruel, ruled Madagascar with an iron fist, fiercely resisting European colonial influence and maintaining the sovereignty and cultural identity of her kingdom. Her reign was marked by both progressive reforms and ruthless policies.

> *"I reign over my own domain and have no desire to become a puppet queen under the protection of a foreign sovereign."*

**Did you know?** Queen Ranavalona I significantly expanded her kingdom's territory during her reign.

## 4 SEPTEMBER

# Margaret Fuller

Women's Rights Advocate and Transcendentalist

1810-1850, USA

A journalist, critic, and women's rights advocate, Margaret Fuller was one of the leading intellectuals of her day. Her book "Woman in the Nineteenth Century" is considered one of the earliest major feminist works in the United States. Fuller was also associated with the transcendentalist movement.

*"Very early, I knew that the only object in life was to grow."*

**Did you know?** Fuller was the first full-time female book reviewer in journalism.

## 5 SEPTEMBER

# Hannah Arendt
Influential Political Theorist

1906-1975, Germany/USA

A political theorist known for her works on totalitarianism and democracy, Hannah Arendt's books, such as "The Human Condition" and "Eichmann in Jerusalem," have had a lasting impact on political philosophy. Her concept of the "banality of evil" is a significant contribution to the understanding of human nature in political crises.

*"The sad truth is that most evil is done by people who never make up their minds to be good or evil."*

**Did you know?** Arendt's coverage of the Eichmann trial for "The New Yorker" stirred much controversy and debate.

## 6 SEPTEMBER

# Mary Wollstonecraft
### Early Feminist Philosopher

1759-1797, United Kingdom

A pioneering advocate for women's rights, Mary Wollstonecraft is best known for her work "A Vindication of the Rights of Woman." In it, she argues for women's education and the recognition of women as individuals, not just mothers and wives.

*"I do not wish them [women] to have power over men; but over themselves."*

**Did you know?** Wollstonecraft's daughter, Mary Shelley, wrote the famous novel "Frankenstein."

## 7 SEPTEMBER

# Assata Shakur

Activist and Icon

1947-Present, USA/Cuba

A member of the Black Panther Party and the Black Liberation Army, Assata Shakur was convicted of a murder she and her supporters claim she did not commit. She escaped prison and was granted asylum in Cuba, where she continues to live. Shakur's autobiography is considered an important work on race and the criminal justice system in America.

*"No one is going to give you the education you need to overthrow them."*

**Did you know?** Shakur was the first woman to be listed on the FBI's Most Wanted Terrorist list.

## 8 SEPTEMBER

# Empress Wei

Empress of the Tang Dynasty

7th century, China

Empress Wei, wife of Emperor Zhongzong of Tang, was known for her ambition and political acumen. After her husband's death, she attempted to take control of the empire by appointing herself as Empress Regent, a bold move in a male-dominated society.

*"In the heart of the palace, the game of power and intrigue unfolds."*

**Did you know?** Empress Wei's reign as Empress Regent was short-lived due to a palace coup.

## 9 SEPTEMBER

# Mother Teresa

Saint of the Gutters

1910-1997, Albania/India

Born in Albania, Mother Teresa dedicated her life to serving the poor in Kolkata, India. She founded the Missionaries of Charity, which continues to provide care for those who have no one else to look after them. Awarded the Nobel Peace Prize, she is revered for her compassion and devotion to the needy.

*"Not all of us can do great things. But we can do small things with great love."*

**Did you know?** Mother Teresa's real name was Anjezë Gonxhe Bojaxhiu.

## 10 SEPTEMBER
# Nadia Comaneci
Olympic Gymnastics Champion

1961-Present, Romania

Nadia Comaneci made history at the 1976 Montreal Olympics by scoring the first perfect 10 in gymnastics. Her performance redefined the sport and made her an international star at just 14 years old.

*"I don't run away from a challenge because I am afraid. Instead, I run toward it because the only way to escape fear is to trample it beneath your feet."*

**Did you know?** Nadia won a total of nine Olympic medals, five of them gold.

## 11 SEPTEMBER

# Queen Esther

Biblical Heroine

Biblical Times, Persia

Queen Esther, a Jewish queen of Persia, is celebrated for her bravery in the Bible. Her story of courage and wisdom is recounted in the Book of Esther, where she risks her life to save her people from a plot to destroy them.

*"For such a time as this, I have been placed upon the throne."*

**Did you know?** The Jewish festival of Purim commemorates the events recounted in the Book of Esther.

## 12 SEPTEMBER

# Julian of Norwich

Medieval Mystic and Theologian

1342-c.1416, United Kingdom

Julian of Norwich was an English mystic known for her theological work, "Revelations of Divine Love," the first book in the English language known to have been written by a woman. Her reflections on God's love and her optimistic theology were groundbreaking for her time.

*"All shall be well, and all shall be well, and all manner of things shall be well."*

**Did you know?** Julian lived most of her life in seclusion as an anchoress (a religious recluse).

## 13 SEPTEMBER

# Maya Angelou

Celebrated Author and Poet

1928-2014, USA

Maya Angelou was an American author, poet, and civil rights activist. Her 1969 memoir, "I Know Why the Caged Bird Sings," made literary history as the first nonfiction bestseller by an African-American woman. Angelou's works are known for their themes of overcoming adversity and the celebration of African-American culture.

*"People will forget what you said, people will forget what you did, but people will never forget how you made them feel."*

**Did you know?** Angelou was also a talented singer and dancer, touring Europe in the 1950s with a production of "Porgy and Bess."

## 14 SEPTEMBER

# Maya Lin

Visionary Artist and Architect

1959-Present, USA

Maya Lin, an American architectural designer and artist, rose to prominence at the age of 21 as the designer of the Vietnam Veterans Memorial in Washington, D.C. Her design, selected from 1,421 entries, was groundbreaking in its simplicity and emotional power. Lin's work, characterized by its environmental focus and minimalist aesthetic, has continued to challenge and inspire, combining art, architecture, and memory with remarkable subtlety and impact.

> *"I try to give people a different way of looking at their surroundings. That's art to me."*

**Did you know?** Lin has designed numerous other significant works, including the Civil Rights Memorial in Montgomery, Alabama.

## 15 SEPTEMBER

# Empress Theodora

Influential Byzantine Empress

c. 500-548, Byzantine Empire

Empress Theodora, wife of Emperor Justinian, was one of the most powerful women in Byzantine history. Rising from humble beginnings, she became an influential figure in the empire's politics. Theodora was a champion of women's rights, passing laws to prohibit trafficking of young girls and altering divorce laws to give more benefits to women.

> *"Never will I allow my pure reputation to be tarnished by an ignoble action."*

**Did you know?** Theodora played a crucial role in quelling the Nika riots, a defining moment in Justinian's reign.

## 16 SEPTEMBER

# Lillian Wald

Nurse and Social Reformer

1867-1940, USA

Lillian Wald, a nurse, and social worker, founded the Henry Street Settlement in New York City, a community center that provided health care, education, and social services to the poor. She was a pioneer in public health nursing and was instrumental in establishing the American Red Cross Nursing Service.

*"The task for the nurse is to provide care, comfort, and counsel to those who cannot, for the time being, do without such service."*

**Did you know?** Wald coined the term "public health nurse" to describe nurses whose work is integrated into the public community.

## 17 SEPTEMBER

# Annie Jump Cannon

Trailblazing Astronomer

1863-1941, USA

An American astronomer, Annie Jump Cannon developed a stellar classification system that became the universal standard. Working at the Harvard College Observatory, Cannon classified around 350,000 stars in her lifetime. Her system, based on the temperature of stars, is still used today.

> *"In the sky, there are always answers and explanations for everything: every pain, every suffering, joy, and confusion."*

**Did you know?** Cannon was deaf for most of her career, which made her achievements even more remarkable.

## 18 SEPTEMBER
# Dorothea Lange
Iconic Photographer of the
American Depression Era

1895-1965, USA

Dorothea Lange was an influential American documentary photographer, best known for her Depression-era work for the Farm Security Administration (FSA). Lange's photographs humanized the tragic consequences of the Great Depression and influenced the development of documentary photography.

*"Photography takes an instant out of time, altering life by holding it still."*

**Did you know?** Lange's most famous photograph, "Migrant Mother," became an icon of the era.

## 19 SEPTEMBER

# Mary Anning
Pioneering Paleontologist

1799-1847, England

Mary Anning was an English fossil collector, dealer, and paleontologist who made key scientific discoveries in the Jurassic marine fossil beds at Lyme Regis. Her findings contributed to important changes in scientific thinking about prehistoric life and the history of the Earth.

*"The world is full of wonders, and each rock may hide a treasure."*

**Did you know?** Anning discovered the first correctly identified ichthyosaur skeleton at the age of 12.

## 20 SEPTEMBER

# Empress Liu Zhi
Compassionate Consort of the Han Dynasty

241-180 BCE, China

Empress Liu Zhi, known for her wisdom and compassion, was an influential figure in the Western Han Dynasty. She was the consort of Emperor Wen and was revered for her role in influencing the emperor towards more benevolent policies and reducing the harshness of punishments.

*"To rule with kindness and benevolence leads to a prosperous realm."*

**Did you know?** Empress Liu Zhi was deeply respected for her role in promoting education and Confucian principles.

## 21 SEPTEMBER

# Murasaki Shikibu

Author of the World's First Novel

c. 973-1014, Japan

Murasaki Shikibu, a lady-in-waiting in the Heian court, is best known as the author of "The Tale of Genji," considered the world's first full-length novel. The book offers a vivid portrayal of court life in classical Japan and is revered for its intricate characterizations and insights into the complexities of human behavior.

*"One ought not to be ashamed of writing if what one writes is worth reading."*

**Did you know?** "The Tale of Genji" was written around the year 1000 and is still celebrated for its literary significance.

## 22 SEPTEMBER
# Mary Leakey
Renowned Paleoanthropologist

1913-1996, England/Kenya

Mary Leakey was a British paleoanthropologist who made several significant discoveries related to the early evolution of humans. Her work in East Africa led to the discovery of the first fossilized Proconsul skull, an extinct ape now believed to be part of the human evolutionary tree.

*"The search for human ancestors begins with a quest for understanding."*

**Did you know?** Mary and her husband Louis Leakey were a formidable team in paleoanthropology.

## 23 SEPTEMBER

# Policarpa Salavarrieta
Heroine of Colombian Independence

1795-1827, Colombia

Policarpa Salavarrieta, commonly known as "La Pola," was a seamstress who spied for the Colombian revolutionary forces during the struggle for independence from Spain. Her intelligence gathering was crucial to the revolution, and she became a symbol of bravery and patriotism.

*"Even if my life ends, the rebellion will go on."*

**Did you know?** "La Pola" was executed for her role in the rebellion, and her last words have become legendary in Colombian history.

## 24 SEPTEMBER

# Joan of Arc
### France's Heroic Saint

c. 1412-1431, France

Joan of Arc, also known as "The Maid of Orléans," is a national heroine of France and a saint of the Catholic Church. At just 17, she led the French army to victory over the English at Orléans, changing the course of the Hundred Years' War. Her vision, courage, and determination made her a legend.

*"I am not afraid... I was born to do this."*

**Did you know?** Joan was canonized as a saint nearly 500 years after her death.

## 25 SEPTEMBER

# Nellie McClung

Canadian Suffragist and Author

1873-1951, Canada

Nellie McClung was a key figure in the Canadian suffrage movement, known for her spirited activism in fighting for women's rights. She played a significant role in the "Persons Case," which ultimately recognized women as "persons" under Canadian law. McClung was also a prolific author, using her writings to advocate for social reform.

*"Never retract, never explain, never apologize. Just get things done and let them howl."*

**Did you know?** McClung was part of "The Famous Five," a group of Canadian women's rights activists.

## 26 SEPTEMBER

# Razia Sultan

First Female Muslim Ruler in South Asia

1205-1240, Delhi Sultanate

Razia Sultan was the first and only female monarch of the Delhi Sultanate. Known for her wisdom, bravery, and just leadership, Razia broke stereotypes in a male-dominated society. She was a skilled administrator and a patron of education and culture.

*"I would rather be remembered as a queen than a woman."*

**Did you know?** Razia Sultan often dressed like a man to establish her authority and lead her army.

## 27 SEPTEMBER

# Rudrama Devi

Warrior Queen of the Kakatiya Dynasty

1259-1289, India

Rudrama Devi, one of the few female rulers in Indian history, effectively governed the Kakatiya dynasty and was known for her administrative and military skills. She adopted male attire and the title of king to assert her authority in a patriarchal society.

*"A queen's duty is to her people, above all else."*

**Did you know?** Rudrama Devi's reign marked a period of prosperity and stability, with significant developments in agriculture and arts.

## 28 SEPTEMBER
# Tsitsi Dangarembga
### Zimbabwean Author and Filmmaker

1959-Present, Zimbabwe

Tsitsi Dangarembga is a notable Zimbabwean author and filmmaker, whose work provides profound insights into African society, especially the lives of women. Her debut novel, "Nervous Conditions," was the first to be published in English by a black Zimbabwean woman and has received international acclaim.

*"At some point, one needs to free oneself from the trauma and victimization of one's past."*

**Did you know?** Dangarembga's novels are part of a trilogy that follows the protagonist, Tambu, through various stages of her life.

## 29 SEPTEMBER

# Leymah Gbowee

Liberian Peace Activist

1972-Present, Liberia

Leymah Gbowee is a Liberian peace activist who played a pivotal role in ending Liberia's Second Civil War in 2003. She organized Christian and Muslim women to demonstrate together, showcasing the power of collaborative peaceful protest.

*"You can never leave footprints that last if you are always walking on tiptoe."*

**Did you know?** Gbowee's efforts were pivotal in electing Ellen Johnson Sirleaf, Africa's first female president.

Activity: Organize a small community event promoting peace and understanding in your neighborhood.

## 30 SEPTEMBER

# Agnes Martin
### Pioneering Abstract Painter

1912-2004, Canada/USA

Agnes Martin was a renowned artist, celebrated for her minimalist and abstract works that convey deep emotion through simple lines and colors. Her work, characterized by serene patterns and subtle variations of form, has had a significant influence on modern art.

*"Beauty is the mystery of life. It is not in the eye, it is in the mind."*

**Did you know?** Martin didn't start painting in her signature style until her 30s, challenging the myth of early success.

# OCTOBER

## 1 OCTOBER

# Juana Azurduy de Padilla

South American Revolutionary Leader

1780-1862, Bolivia/Argentina

A fearless leader in the South American struggle for independence, Juana Azurduy de Padilla fought against Spanish rule. She commanded a military unit of indigenous men and women, known for her bravery and brilliant tactics.

> *"I have lived for freedom, I have tried to find the freedom of my spirit in the fight for liberation."*

**Did you know?** Juana was promoted to the rank of Lieutenant Colonel by Simon Bolivar himself.

## 2 OCTOBER

# Marie Stopes
Pioneer in Family Planning

1880-1958, United Kingdom

Marie Stopes was a British author, paleobotanist, and campaigner for women's rights. She made significant contributions to plant paleontology and coal classification, and was the first to open a birth control clinic in Britain.

*"No woman can call herself free who does not own and control her body."*

**Did you know?** Stopes' controversial book, "Married Love," was one of the first texts to discuss birth control openly.

## 3 OCTOBER

# Rosalind Elsie Franklin

Pioneering X-ray Crystallographer

1920-1958, United Kingdom

Rosalind Franklin was an English chemist whose work on X-ray diffraction was critical in understanding the molecular structures of DNA. Her photographs of DNA led to the discovery of its double helix structure, although her contributions were largely recognized posthumously.

*"Science and everyday life cannot and should not be separated."*

**Did you know?** Franklin also made significant contributions to the understanding of viruses and RNA.

## 4 OCTOBER
# Phyllis Wheatley
First African American Female Poet

c. 1753-1784, USA

Phyllis Wheatley was the first African American woman to publish a book of poetry. Enslaved and brought to America, she was educated by her owners and began writing poetry, eventually gaining fame for her eloquent words that transcended the boundaries of race and gender in colonial America.

> *"In every human Breast, God has implanted a Principle, which we call Love of Freedom; it is impatient of Oppression, and pants for Deliverance."*

**Did you know?** Wheatley wrote a poem for George Washington, who invited her to his home as thanks.

## 5 OCTOBER

# Clara Schumann

Renowned Pianist and Composer

1819-1896, Germany

Clara Schumann was a distinguished pianist of the Romantic era and an accomplished composer, known for her interpretations of her husband Robert Schumann and Johannes Brahms' works. She was one of the first pianists to perform from memory, setting a standard still followed today.

> *"Music is the language of the spirit. It opens the secret of life, bringing peace, abolishing strife."*

**Did you know?** Clara juggled her career with raising a large family and managing her husband's mental illness.

## 6 OCTOBER

# Georgia O'Keeffe
Pioneering American Artist

1887-1986, USA

Georgia O'Keeffe, one of the most significant artists of the 20th century, is known for her unique and captivating depictions of flowers, skyscrapers, and southwestern landscapes. Her innovative style defied the norms of her time and opened new paths in the world of modern art. O'Keeffe's bold use of colors and abstraction made her a pioneering figure in the American modernist movement.

*"I've been absolutely terrified every moment of my life, and I've never let it keep me from doing a single thing I wanted to do."*

**Did you know?** O'Keeffe was awarded the Presidential Medal of Freedom and the National Medal of Arts.

## 7 OCTOBER

# Emmeline Pankhurst

Leader of the British Suffragette Movement

1858-1928, United Kingdom

Emmeline Pankhurst was a key figure in the fight for women's suffrage in Britain. She founded the Women's Social and Political Union (WSPU), known for its militant tactics, including hunger strikes and civil disobedience. Pankhurst's unwavering dedication played a pivotal role in women gaining the right to vote.

*"Deeds, not words, was to be our permanent motto."*

**Did you know?** Time named her one of the 100 Most Important People of the 20th Century.

## 8 OCTOBER

# La Malinche

Interpreter and Advisor in the Spanish Conquest of Mexico

c. 1500-1529, Mexico

La Malinche, born Malinalli, played a crucial role in the Spanish conquest of the Aztec Empire as an interpreter, advisor, and intermediary for the Spanish conquistador, Hernán Cortés. She was fluent in Nahuatl and Maya languages, and learned Spanish quickly, becoming an invaluable asset in negotiations.

*"I am both a bridge and a barrier between two worlds."*

**Did you know?** La Malinche's role is complex; she's viewed as both a traitorous figure and a victim of her circumstances.

## 9 OCTOBER

# Claribel Cone

Patron of Modern Art and Medicine

1864-1929, USA

Claribel Cone, along with her sister Etta, amassed one of the world's most significant collections of modern art. A respected physician and pathologist, Claribel balanced her medical career with her passion for art, supporting and befriending many avant-garde artists in Europe.

*"Art is the eternal seeking of truth, through beauty and understanding."*

**Did you know?** The Cone Collection, now housed in the Baltimore Museum of Art, includes works by Matisse, Picasso, and Cézanne.

## 10 OCTOBER
# Qiu Jin
Chinese Revolutionary and Feminist

1875-1907, China

Qiu Jin was a Chinese revolutionary, writer, and feminist. She was an outspoken advocate for women's rights, calling for an end to practices like foot binding and the oppressive Qing dynasty. Qiu Jin was executed for her role in a failed uprising, becoming a martyr and symbol of women's independence in China.

*"Do not tell me women are not the stuff of heroes."*

**Did you know?** Qiu Jin was also known as the "Woman Knight of Mirror Lake."

## 11 OCTOBER

# Rita Levi-Montalcini
Nobel Laureate in Physiology or Medicine

1909-2012, Italy

Rita Levi-Montalcini was an Italian neurobiologist who, along with colleague Stanley Cohen, received the Nobel Prize for their discovery of nerve growth factor. Despite facing anti-Semitic laws and World War II disruptions, she conducted groundbreaking research on cell growth.

*"Above all, don't fear difficult moments. The best comes from them."*

**Did you know?** Levi-Montalcini was appointed a Senator for Life in the Italian Senate in 2001.

## 12 OCTOBER

# Helen Keller

Advocate for the Disabled

1880-1968, USA

Despite losing her sight and hearing at a young age, Helen Keller became an iconic advocate for people with disabilities. With the help of her teacher, Anne Sullivan, Keller learned to communicate and went on to become a prolific author, lecturer, and activist.

*"The only thing worse than being blind is having sight but no vision."*

**Did you know?** Keller was the first deaf-blind person to earn a Bachelor of Arts degree.

## 13 OCTOBER

# Queen Victoria

Longest-Reigning Monarch of Britain

1819-1901, United Kingdom

Queen Victoria, who reigned for 63 years, oversaw a period of industrial, cultural, political, scientific, and military change in the United Kingdom, and the expansion of the British Empire. Her era was marked by progress and innovation.

*"Great events make me quiet and calm; it is only trifles that irritate my nerves."*

**Did you know?** The Victorian Era was named after her and is associated with Britain's greatest age of industrial, cultural, and imperial expansion.

## 14 OCTOBER

# Noor Inayat Khan

WWII Spy and Heroine

1914-1944, France/United Kingdom

Noor Inayat Khan served as a wireless operator for the British in Nazi-occupied France during World War II. Despite being captured and executed by the Gestapo, her courage and refusal to betray her colleagues made her one of the war's most revered heroines.

*"I wish some Indians would win high military distinction in this war. It would help to build a bridge between the English people and the Indians."*

**Did you know?** Inayat Khan was posthumously awarded the George Cross, the highest civilian decoration in the United Kingdom.

## 15 OCTOBER

# Fannie Lou Hamer

Civil Rights Activist

1917-1977, USA

Fannie Lou Hamer was a key figure in the Civil Rights Movement, known for her powerful speeches and activism. Despite facing violence and intimidation, she fought tirelessly for African American voting rights and co-founded the Mississippi Freedom Democratic Party.

*"I am sick and tired of being sick and tired."*

**Did you know?** Hamer's testimony at the 1964 Democratic National Convention brought national attention to the civil rights struggle in the South.

## 16 OCTOBER

# Queen Liliuokalani
Last Sovereign Monarch of Hawaii

1838-1917, Hawaii

Queen Liliuokalani was the last reigning monarch of the Kingdom of Hawaii. Known for her determination to maintain Hawaiian sovereignty against annexation by the United States, she faced overthrow by U.S. interests and was placed under house arrest. Her legacy is remembered for her efforts to preserve Hawaiian culture and autonomy.

*"Hawaii's own true sons, be loyal to your chief. Your country's liege and lord, the Alii."*

**Did you know?** Liliuokalani was also a composer and wrote the famous Hawaiian song, "Aloha 'Oe."

## 17 OCTOBER

# Queen Shirin

Influential Persian Queen

630-705, Persia

Queen Shirin, also known as Shirin the Fair, was the Christian wife of Khosrow II, the last great king of the Sasanian Empire. Famed for her beauty and intelligence, Shirin had a significant influence on Persian culture and politics. Her legendary love story with Khosrow II has been immortalized in Persian literature, notably by the poet Nezami Ganjavi.

*"Love and compassion are necessities, not luxuries. Without them, humanity cannot survive."*

**Did you know?** Shirin is often celebrated for her patronage of art and architecture, including constructing palaces and churches.

## 18 OCTOBER

# Mileva Marić

Einstein's Collaborator and Physicist

1875-1948, Serbia/Switzerland

Mileva Marić was a Serbian physicist and mathematician and the first wife of Albert Einstein. She was one of the few women to study at the Zurich Polytechnic at that time. While her contributions to Einstein's work remain a subject of debate, many believe she played a significant role in his early scientific achievements.

*"I am happy when I can contribute to the great work of research."*

**Did you know?** Marić co-authored a paper with Einstein, which led to the development of the special theory of relativity.

## 19 OCTOBER

# Harriet Beecher Stowe

Author of 'Uncle Tom's Cabin'

1811-1896, USA

Harriet Beecher Stowe was an American abolitionist and author, best known for her novel "Uncle Tom's Cabin." This influential book depicted the harsh realities of slavery and galvanized anti-slavery sentiments in the North, significantly impacting American public opinion and the abolitionist movement.

*"The longest way must have its close - the gloomiest night will wear on to a morning."*

**Did you know?** "Uncle Tom's Cabin" was the best-selling novel of the 19th century and the second best-selling book, following the Bible.

## 20 OCTOBER

# Jane Jacobs
Urbanist and Activist

1916-2006, USA/Canada

Jane Jacobs was a writer, urbanist, and activist best known for her influence on urban studies. Her book, "The Death and Life of Great American Cities," argued that urban renewal did not respect the needs of city dwellers. Jacobs championed a community-based approach to city building and was instrumental in preserving many historic New York City neighborhoods.

*"Cities have the capability of providing something for everybody, only because, and only when, they are created by everybody."*

**Did you know?** Jacobs was instrumental in the cancellation of the Lower Manhattan Expressway, which would have passed through Greenwich Village and SoHo.

## 21 OCTOBER

# Bertha von Suttner

Nobel Peace Laureate

1843-1914, Austria

Bertha von Suttner was an Austrian-Bohemian pacifist and novelist. She was the first woman to be awarded the Nobel Peace Prize and was influential in the formation of the international peace movement. Her novel, "Lay Down Your Arms," powerfully advocated for peace and disarmament.

*"The movement for the abolition of war is bound to win. It needs only to be understood."*

**Did you know?** von Suttner significantly influenced Alfred Nobel's decision to include a peace prize among the Nobel Prizes.

## 22 OCTOBER
# Rachel Carson
Environmental Pioneer

1907-1964, USA

Rachel Carson was a marine biologist, author, and conservationist whose book "Silent Spring" is credited with advancing the global environmental movement. Her work brought attention to the dangers of chemical pesticides and inspired an ecological consciousness.

*"The more clearly we can focus our attention on the wonders and realities of the universe about us, the less taste we shall have for destruction."*

**Did you know?** "Silent Spring" led to a nationwide ban on DDT and other pesticides and inspired the creation of the U.S. Environmental Protection Agency.

## 23 OCTOBER

# Henrietta Swan Leavitt

Pioneer in Astronomy

1868-1921, USA

Henrietta Swan Leavitt was an American astronomer whose discoveries led to the first method of measuring distances beyond our solar system. Working at the Harvard College Observatory, Leavitt discovered the relation between the luminosity and the period of Cepheid variable stars, a key to determining cosmic distances.

> *"Astronomy compels the soul to look upwards and leads us from this world to another."*

**Did you know?** Leavitt's work laid the foundation for Edwin Hubble's discovery that the universe is expanding.

## 24 OCTOBER

# Mary Shelley

Author of 'Frankenstein'

1797-1851, United Kingdom

Mary Shelley was an English novelist best known for her novel "Frankenstein," widely considered the first science fiction novel. Written when she was just 18, the book explores themes of creation, responsibility, and the limits of scientific endeavor.

*"Beware; for I am fearless, and therefore powerful."*

**Did you know?** "Frankenstein" was initially published anonymously, and many assumed the author was Percy Shelley, her husband.

## 25 OCTOBER

# Queen Arwa bint Ahmad

### Yemen's Influential Ruler

1048-1138, Yemen

Queen Arwa bint Ahmad was the long-reigning and much-celebrated ruler of Yemen. Known for her wisdom, piety, and dedication to her people, she was one of the few female Islamic rulers. Queen Arwa's administration was marked by stability, prosperity, and architectural development.

> *"To serve with justice is the highest form of devotion."*

**Did you know?** Queen Arwa was known for her intelligence and was well-versed in the Quran and Hadith.

## 26 OCTOBER
# Josephine Baker
Entertainer and Civil Rights Activist

1906-1975, USA/France

Josephine Baker was an American-born French entertainer, resistance agent, and civil rights activist. Known for her charismatic stage presence and groundbreaking performances, Baker was also a dedicated advocate for civil rights, refusing to perform for segregated audiences.

*"The things we truly love stay with us always, locked in our hearts as long as life remains."*

**Did you know?** Baker was the first African American woman to star in a major motion picture, "Zouzou."

## 27 OCTOBER

# Rosa Luxemburg
Revolutionary and Martyr

1871-1919, Poland/Germany

Rosa Luxemburg was a Marxist theorist, philosopher, economist, anti-war activist, and revolutionary socialist of Polish-Jewish descent. A key figure in the German Spartacist uprising, Luxemburg's writings on class struggle and socialism have been influential in leftist movements.

*"Freedom is always the freedom of the one who thinks differently."*

**Did you know?** Luxemburg's murder in 1919 made her a martyr for the socialist cause.

## 28 OCTOBER

# Gerty Cori

Biochemist and Nobel Laureate

1896-1957, Czech Republic/USA

Gerty Cori was a Czech-American biochemist who, along with her husband Carl Cori, won the Nobel Prize in Physiology or Medicine for their discovery of the course of the catalytic conversion of glycogen. She was the first woman to win the Nobel Prize in this category.

*"In science, one must start with certainties; in life, with uncertainties."*

**Did you know?** The Cori cycle, an important biochemical pathway, was named after her and her husband.

## 29 OCTOBER

# Gertrude Bell

Adventurer, Diplomat, and Archaeologist

1868-1926, United Kingdom

Gertrude Bell was an English writer, traveler, political officer, administrator, and archaeologist who played a significant role in establishing and administering the modern state of Iraq. Known for her extensive travels in Arabia, she was instrumental in British imperial policy-making.

*"I have seldom met a more fascinating personality."*

**Did you know?** Bell's extensive travels in the Middle East led her to be called the "female Lawrence of Arabia."

## 30 OCTOBER

# Marjory Stoneman Douglas
Environmentalist and Author

1890-1998, USA

Marjory Stoneman Douglas was an American journalist, writer, feminist, and environmentalist known for her staunch defense of the Everglades against efforts to drain it and reclaim land for development. Her book, "The Everglades: River of Grass," redefined the perception of the Everglades as a treasured river instead of a worthless swamp.

*"Be a nuisance where it counts; do your part to inform and stimulate the public to join your action."*

**Did you know?** Douglas lived to be 108 and was active in environmental causes almost until her death.

## 31 OCTOBER

# Beryl Markham

Trailblazing Aviator and Author

1902-1986, Kenya/UK

Beryl Markham, a British-born Kenyan, was a pioneering aviator, adventurer, and racehorse trainer. She was the first woman to fly solo across the Atlantic from east to west. Her memoir, "West with the Night," recounts her remarkable adventures in Africa and her historic flight, highlighting her fearless spirit and love for Africa.

*"Success breeds confidence."*

**Did you know?** Markham's flight made international headlines, but her book became famous much later, rediscovered in the 1980s.

365 INSPIRING WOMEN

# NOVEMBER

## 1 NOVEMBER

# Nellie Bly

Pioneering Investigative Journalist

1864-1922, USA

Nellie Bly was a groundbreaking American journalist known for her investigative and undercover reporting. She famously traveled around the world in 72 days, breaking the fictional record in Jules Verne's novel. Bly also feigned insanity to report on the conditions in a mental institution from the inside.

*"Energy rightly applied and directed will accomplish anything."*

**Did you know?** Bly's report from the asylum brought about significant reforms in mental health care.

## 2 NOVEMBER

# Margaret Sanger

Birth Control Activist and Nurse

1879-1966, USA

Margaret Sanger was a nurse and the leading advocate of the birth control movement in the United States. She opened the first birth control clinic in the U.S. and established organizations that evolved into the Planned Parenthood Federation of America.

*"No woman can call herself free who does not own and control her body."*

**Did you know?** Sanger's work faced strong opposition, but she continued her advocacy, changing public perceptions on birth control.

## 3 NOVEMBER

# Emmy Noether
Pioneering Mathematician

1882-1935, Germany/USA

Emmy Noether, one of the most important mathematicians of her time, made groundbreaking contributions to abstract algebra and theoretical physics. Her work on symmetries in physics, known as Noether's Theorem, is fundamental in modern physics.

> *"My methods are really methods of working and thinking; this is why they have crept in everywhere anonymously."*

**Did you know?** Noether overcame barriers in academia due to her gender, working at universities without pay.

## 4 NOVEMBER
# Savitribai Phule
Social Reformer and Educator

1831-1897, India

Savitribai Phule was a pioneering Indian feminist, educator, and social reformer. Along with her husband, Jyotirao Phule, she played an important role in improving women's rights in India. She is regarded as the first female teacher in India and opened the first school for girls.

*"To educate women is to educate a whole nation."*

**Did you know?** Phule and her husband founded the Satyashodhak Samaj, a society promoting equal rights for marginalized people.

## 5 NOVEMBER

# Edith Wharton

Pulitzer Prize-Winning Author

1862-1937, USA/France

Edith Wharton was a prominent American novelist and the first woman to win the Pulitzer Prize for Fiction. Her novels and short stories are known for their witty examination of upper-class society in the late 19th and early 20th centuries. "The Age of Innocence" is one of her most famous works.

> *"There are two ways of spreading light: to be the candle or the mirror that reflects it."*

**Did you know?** Wharton was also a garden designer and interior decorator.

## 6 NOVEMBER

# Septima Poinsette Clark
Educator and Civil Rights Activist

1898-1987, USA

Septima Poinsette Clark, often called the "Mother of the Civil Rights Movement," was an educator and a civil rights activist. Her citizenship schools helped enfranchise and empower African Americans in the South during the Civil Rights Movement.

*"Knowledge could empower marginalized groups in ways that formal legal equality couldn't."*

**Did you know?** Clark's work inspired Rosa Parks and Martin Luther King Jr.

## 7 NOVEMBER

# Chien-Shiung Wu

Pioneering Experimental Physicist

1912-1997, China/USA

Chien-Shiung Wu was a Chinese-American experimental physicist who made significant contributions in the field of nuclear physics. Wu worked on the Manhattan Project and her experiments disproved the Law of Conservation of Parity, changing our understanding of physics.

*"I wonder whether the tiny atoms and nuclei, or the mathematical symbols, or the DNA molecules have any preference for either masculine or feminine treatment."*

**Did you know?** Despite her contributions, Wu was often overlooked for awards in favor of her male colleagues.

## 8 NOVEMBER

# Empress Dowager Cixi
Influential Chinese Ruler

1835-1908, China

Empress Dowager Cixi was one of the most powerful women in the history of China. Starting as a concubine, she rose to become the de facto ruler of China for almost half a century. Her rule, controversial and often misunderstood, was marked by both modernization efforts and a resistance to foreign influence.

*"I have no desire but to prevent foreign powers from dividing up China and treat it like a melon."*

**Did you know?** Cixi initiated reforms in the Qing dynasty, including the modernization of the military, industry, and railways.

## 9 NOVEMBER

# Hrotsvitha

First Known Female Playwright

c. 935-c. 1002, Germany

Hrotsvitha of Gandersheim, a German secular canoness, poet, and playwright, is considered the first known female playwright. She wrote plays, poems, and legends during the Ottonian dynasty, challenging the traditional roles of women in the arts.

*"Stronger than a man, simpler than a child, her nature stood."*

**Did you know?** Hrotsvitha's plays were modeled on the works of Roman playwright Terence but had Christian themes.

## 10 NOVEMBER

# Dian Fossey

Primatologist and Conservationist

1932-1985, Rwanda

Dian Fossey was an American primatologist and conservationist known for her extensive study of mountain gorillas in Rwanda. Her efforts to protect the gorillas from poaching and habitat loss had a lasting impact on conservation. Fossey's work was famously chronicled in her book "Gorillas in the Mist."

*"When you realize the value of all life, you dwell less on what is past and concentrate more on the preservation of the future."*

**Did you know?** Fossey's aggressive conservation tactics were controversial but effective in curbing poaching.

## 11 NOVEMBER

# Lady Fu Hao

Powerful Shang Dynasty Military Leader

c. 1200 BCE, China

Lady Fu Hao was a Shang dynasty queen and military general under King Wu Ding. She led numerous military campaigns and was also a high priestess known for her ritualistic activities. Her tomb, one of the best-preserved from the Shang dynasty, revealed her status and power.

> *"In the echoes of ancient bronze and jade, the strength of a woman warrior endures."*

**Did you know?** Lady Fu Hao's tomb contained weapons, suggesting her role as a military leader.

## 12 NOVEMBER

# Triaria

Influential Woman of Ancient Rome

1st Century BCE, Rome

Triaria, a lesser-known yet influential figure in Roman history, was the wife of Lucius Vitellius, a governor under Emperor Nero. Not much is known about her life, but ancient texts suggest she wielded considerable influence in her husband's political affairs and was noted for her assertive personality, a rarity for women in Roman society.

*"Influence often lies where we least expect it."*

**Did you know?** Triaria's assertiveness was noted by historians as unusual and noteworthy for a woman of her time.

## 13 NOVEMBER

# Tarabai Bhonsle

### Warrior Queen of the Maratha Empire

1675-1761, India

Tarabai Bhonsle was a regent of the Maratha empire in India. Following the death of her husband, Rajaram Chhatrapati, she led her kingdom against the Mughal Empire with remarkable skill. Tarabai was known for her administrative genius and her ability to maintain Maratha resistance against Mughal invasion.

*"A kingdom knows no gender, only strength."*

**Did you know?** Tarabai continued to be a significant figure in Maratha politics well into her sixties.

## 14 NOVEMBER
# Elizabeth Blackwell
First Woman to Receive a Medical Degree in the United States

1821-1910, USA

Elizabeth Blackwell was a trailblazing figure in medicine, becoming the first woman in the United States to earn a medical degree. She faced significant obstacles in her pursuit of medical education but persevered and opened new paths for women in the medical profession.

*"I do not wish to give women a first place, still less a second one, but the complete freedom to take their true place whatever it may be."*

**Did you know?** Blackwell also helped establish the New York Infirmary for Women and Children.

## 15 NOVEMBER

# Octavia E. Butler

Visionary Science Fiction Writer

1947-2006, USA

Octavia E. Butler was an African American author known for her science fiction novels and short stories. Her work explores themes of race, gender, and humanity, often delving into futuristic and speculative fiction. Butler's unique voice and imaginative storytelling won her multiple Hugo and Nebula awards.

*"In order to rise from its own ashes, a Phoenix first must burn."*

**Did you know?** Butler's novel "Kindred" is a cornerstone of speculative fiction, combining elements of science fiction with African American history.

## 16 NOVEMBER

# Sylvia Earle

Renowned Marine Biologist and Oceanographer

1935-Present, USA

Sylvia Earle is a prominent marine biologist, oceanographer, and explorer known for her research on marine algae and her advocacy for ocean conservation. She was the first female chief scientist of the U.S. National Oceanic and Atmospheric Administration and has led more than a hundred underwater expeditions.

*"The more you know, the more you care...the more you care, the more you do."*

**Did you know?** Earle was named Time Magazine's first Hero for the Planet in 1998.

## 17 NOVEMBER

# Alice Ball

Pioneer in Leprosy Treatment

1892-1916, USA

Alice Ball, an African American chemist, developed the first effective treatment for leprosy. Her method, known as the "Ball Method," was a significant breakthrough and continued to be used for over two decades to treat Hansen's disease (leprosy).

> *"Lasting change happens when people see for themselves that a different way of life is more fulfilling than their present one."*

**Did you know?** Ball's research was only properly credited to her after her death.

## 18 NOVEMBER
# Maria Goeppert Mayer
Nobel Laureate in Physics

1906-1972, Germany/USA

Maria Goeppert Mayer, a German-American theoretical physicist, won the Nobel Prize in Physics for her development of the nuclear shell model of the atomic nucleus. She was the second female Nobel laureate in physics, after Marie Curie.

*"I was taught that the way of progress was neither swift nor easy."*

**Did you know?** Mayer's work was crucial in the development of the atomic bomb during World War II.

## 19 NOVEMBER

# Empress Guanglie

Influential Chinese Empress of the Ming Dynasty

15th Century, China

Empress Guanglie, also known as Empress Xiaogongzhang, was an empress of the Ming Dynasty known for her wisdom, compassion, and influence in state affairs. She played a significant role in the administration of the empire and in promoting education and Confucian values.

*"A wise ruler listens and learns from their people."*

**Did you know?** Empress Guanglie was known for her charitable works and efforts to improve the lives of the people.

## 20 NOVEMBER

# Empress Wu Zetian
### The Only Female Emperor of China

624-705, China

Wu Zetian was the only female emperor in the history of China, ruling during the Tang Dynasty. She rose from a concubine to the empress and eventually became the de facto ruler. Her reign was marked by a mix of ruthlessness and progress, including improvements in government and expansion of the empire.

*"To rule is to be in solitude, above all when one is a woman."*

**Did you know?** Wu Zetian also promoted education and literature, commissioning biographies of prominent women.

## 21 NOVEMBER

# Elizabeth Fry

Prison Reformer and Social Activist

1780-1845, United Kingdom

Elizabeth Fry was an English prison reformer, social activist, and a key figure in the British humanitarian movement. Known as the "angel of prisons," she was instrumental in improving conditions for women in prisons and advocating for their rights.

*"Punishment is not for revenge, but to lessen crime and reform the criminal."*

**Did you know?** Fry was depicted on the British £5 note, honoring her contributions to society.

## 22 NOVEMBER

# Hypatia of Alexandria
Renowned Philosopher and Mathematician

c. 360-415, Egypt

Hypatia of Alexandria was a Greek mathematician, philosopher, and astronomer in Egypt. She was a leading figure in the Hellenistic world and one of the first women to make significant contributions to the development of mathematics and philosophy.

*"Reserve your right to think, for even to think wrongly is better than not to think at all."*

**Did you know?** Hypatia was known for her work on the development of the astrolabe.

## 23 NOVEMBER

# Taytu Betul

Empress of Ethiopia and Military Strategist

c.1851-1918, Ethiopia

Empress Taytu Betul was the wife of Emperor Menelik II of Ethiopia and played a key role in maintaining Ethiopian independence during a period of heightened European colonial expansion in Africa. She was a skilled military strategist and diplomat.

*"Wisdom is not like money to be tied up and hidden."*

**Did you know?** Taytu Betul led troops in the Battle of Adwa, one of the first victories of African forces over a European colonial power.

## 24 NOVEMBER

# Margaret Atwood

Prolific Author and Poet

1939-Present, Canada

Margaret Atwood is a Canadian poet, novelist, literary critic, essayist, and environmental activist. She is best known for her profound and thought-provoking novels, including "The Handmaid's Tale," which has become a symbol of women's struggle against repression. Atwood's work often focuses on themes of gender and identity, the environment, and the power dynamics within society.

*"A word after a word after a word is power."*

**Did you know?** Atwood is also a co-founder of the Griffin Poetry Prize and the Writers' Trust of Canada.

## 25 NOVEMBER

# Mabel Ping-Hua Lee

Suffragist and Advocate for Women's Rights

1896-1966, USA

Mabel Ping-Hua Lee was a Chinese-American women's rights activist known for her efforts in the women's suffrage movement in the United States. Despite being unable to vote herself due to the Chinese Exclusion Act, Lee was a powerful advocate for women's suffrage and dedicated her life to promoting education and equal rights.

> *"The welfare of China and possibly its very existence as an independent nation depend on the winning of equal rights and opportunities for Chinese women."*

**Did you know?** Lee was the first Chinese woman to earn a Ph.D. in Economics from Columbia University.

## 26 NOVEMBER
# J.K. Rowling
Beloved Author of the Harry Potter Series

1965-Present, United Kingdom

J.K. Rowling is a British author, philanthropist, film producer, television producer, and screenwriter best known for writing the Harry Potter fantasy series. The books have gained immense popularity, won multiple awards, and sold more than 500 million copies worldwide, becoming the best-selling book series in history. Rowling's story from struggling single mother to a bestselling author is as inspiring as her novels.

*"It is our choices, Harry, that show what we truly are, far more than our abilities."*

**Did you know?** Rowling's first Harry Potter book was rejected by several publishers before it was finally accepted.

## 27 NOVEMBER

# Ella Fitzgerald

Legendary Jazz Singer

1917-1996, USA

Ella Fitzgerald, known as the "First Lady of Song," was an American jazz singer famous for her pure, impeccable voice and her ability to improvise, particularly in scat singing. Fitzgerald had a remarkable range and a vocal style that delighted audiences and won her 13 Grammy awards and the Presidential Medal of Freedom.

*"The only thing better than singing is more singing."*

**Did you know?** Fitzgerald was also known for her collaborations with other jazz legends like Louis Armstrong and Duke Ellington.

## 28 NOVEMBER

# Olive Schreiner
Writer and Feminist Pioneer

1855-1920, South Africa

Olive Schreiner was a South African author, anti-war campaigner, and intellectual. She is best remembered for her novel "The Story of an African Farm," which dealt with themes of feminism, free thought, and the injustice of racial inequality. Schreiner was a powerful advocate for women's rights and a critic of the rigid societal norms of her time.

*"I am not an angel, nor a genie, nor a ghost...I am a woman."*

**Did you know?** Schreiner's work influenced later generations of feminists, including Simone de Beauvoir.

## 29 NOVEMBER

# Agatha Christie
The Queen of Mystery

1890-1976, United Kingdom

Agatha Christie was an English writer known for her sixty-six detective novels and fourteen short story collections, particularly those revolving around her fictional detectives Hercule Poirot and Miss Marple. Christie has been called the "Queen of Mystery," and her books have sold over a billion copies in English and another billion in a multitude of foreign languages.

*"The impossible could not have happened, therefore the impossible must be possible in spite of appearances."*

**Did you know?** Christie also wrote the world's longest-running play, "The Mousetrap."

## 30 NOVEMBER

# Gauri Ma

Indian Social Reformer and Champion
of Women's Rights

1857-1938, India

Gauri Ma was an influential figure in India's social reform movement, particularly in advocating for the rights and welfare of women. A disciple of Sri Ramakrishna, she dedicated her life to the upliftment of women, especially widows, establishing one of the earliest schools for girls in Bengal.

*"Uplifting the status of women is essential for the progress of our country."*

**Did you know?** Gauri Ma faced significant opposition from conservative sections of society but remained steadfast in her mission.

# DECEMBER

## 1 DECEMBER

# Margaret Heafield Hamilton

Computer Scientist and Software Engineering Pioneer

1936-Present, USA

Margaret Heafield Hamilton is a computer scientist and systems engineer who played a crucial role in the development of software for NASA's Apollo missions. Her work on the onboard flight software for the Apollo spacecraft was instrumental in the success of the first moon landing. Hamilton's approach to software engineering laid the groundwork for many modern methods in the field.

*"The most important thing I accomplished, other than building the algorithms, was to make it reliable, to not fail."*

**Did you know?** Hamilton coined the term "software engineering" to give software its due, alongside the hardware development.

## 2 DECEMBER

# Yayoi Kusama

Influential Japanese Contemporary Artist

1929-Present, Japan

Yayoi Kusama is a Japanese contemporary artist known for her extensive use of polka dots and for her immersive, large-scale installations. Her work transcends the traditional boundaries of painting, sculpture, and installations, often incorporating elements of her own psychological experiences.

*"I convert the energy of life into dots of the universe... they are a way to infinity."*

**Did you know?** Kusama has voluntarily lived in a psychiatric hospital since the 1970s, where she has continued to create art.

## 3 DECEMBER

# Edmonia Lewis

Pioneering African American and Native American Sculptor

c. 1844-1907, USA

Edmonia Lewis was the first African American and Native American woman to gain fame and recognition as a sculptor. Working in Rome for most of her career, her work blended themes from her African American and Ojibwa heritage, focusing on figures from history and legend.

*"I have a strong sympathy for all women who have struggled and suffered."*

**Did you know?** Lewis's work "The Death of Cleopatra" was showcased at the 1876 Centennial Exposition in Philadelphia.

## 4 DECEMBER

# Nur Jahan
Influential Empress of the Mughal Empire

1577-1645, India

Nur Jahan was the twentieth and most beloved wife of the Mughal Emperor Jahangir. She is often considered the real power behind the throne, significantly influencing the politics, culture, and architecture of the Mughal era. An accomplished poet and a patron of the arts, she was also known for her exceptional beauty and intelligence.

*"Power and beauty must not be dissociated in the mind of a woman."*

**Did you know?** Nur Jahan was one of the few women in history to issue imperial orders, known as Nur Jahan's Orders.

## 5 DECEMBER

# Bartolina Sisa

Indigenous Aymara Leader and Revolutionary

c. 1750-1782, Bolivia

Bartolina Sisa was an Aymara leader who fought against Spanish colonial rule in Bolivia. Alongside her husband, Tupac Katari, she led a siege on La Paz, asserting indigenous rights and resistance. She is remembered for her courage and leadership in the face of oppression.

*"I will return and be millions."*

**Did you know?** Bartolina Sisa is commemorated every year on September 5th, known as Bartolina Sisa Day.

## 6 DECEMBER

# Constance Markievicz

Irish Revolutionary and Politician

1868-1927, Ireland

Constance Markievicz was an Irish revolutionary, suffragist, and the first woman elected to the British House of Commons. A key figure in the 1916 Easter Rising, she was a passionate advocate for Irish independence and women's rights.

*"We went out to fight for Ireland and for freedom."*

**Did you know?** Markievicz was the first woman in Europe to hold a cabinet position (Minister for Labour of the Irish Republic, 1919-1922).

## 7 DECEMBER
# Barbara Walters
Trailblazing Television Journalist

1929-Present, USA

Barbara Walters is an American broadcast journalist, author, and television personality. She is known for her interviewing abilities and was the first woman to co-anchor a network evening news program. Throughout her career, Walters interviewed many key figures and was a pioneer for women in journalism.

> *"To feel valued, to know, even if only once in a while, that you can do a job well is an absolutely marvelous feeling."*

**Did you know?** Walters has interviewed every American president and first lady since Richard Nixon.

## 8 DECEMBER
# Sayyida al Hurra
Pirate Queen of the Mediterranean

c. 1485-1561, Morocco

Sayyida al Hurra was a pirate queen who ruled the western Mediterranean Sea for over two decades during the early 16th century. She was also the last woman to hold the title of "al Hurra" (Queen) in Islamic history. Her fleet dominated the waters, and she was known for her alliance with the famous pirate Barbarossa.

*"Revenge was a music I played with joy."*

**Did you know?** Sayyida's piracy was partly motivated by revenge against the Portuguese, who had disrupted her life when she was young.

## 9 DECEMBER

# Kate Sheppard

Leader of the Women's Suffrage Movement in New Zealand

1847-1934, New Zealand

Kate Sheppard was the most prominent member of the women's suffrage movement in New Zealand and the country's most famous suffragette. Because of her efforts, New Zealand became the first country to grant women the right to vote in 1893.

*"All that separates, whether of race, class, creed, or sex, is inhuman, and must be overcome."*

**Did you know?** Sheppard's image appears on the New Zealand ten-dollar note.

## 10 DECEMBER

# Katharine Hepburn

Iconic American Actress

1907-2003, USA

Katharine Hepburn was a leading lady in Hollywood for more than 60 years. She received four Academy Awards for Best Actress—a record for any performer. Hepburn was known for her fierce independence, spirited personality, and pioneering role in changing the perception of women in Hollywood.

*"If you obey all the rules, you miss all the fun."*

**Did you know?** Hepburn often wore trousers before they became fashionable for women, contributing to significant changes in women's fashion.

## 11 DECEMBER

# Sarah Breedlove (Madam C.J. Walker)

First Female Self-Made Millionaire in America

1867-1919, USA

Sarah Breedlove, known as Madam C.J. Walker, was an African American entrepreneur, philanthropist, and political and social activist. She is recorded as the first female self-made millionaire in America in the Guinness Book of World Records. Walker made her fortune by developing and marketing a line of beauty and hair products for black women.

> *"I had to make my own living and my own opportunity. But I made it! Don't sit down and wait for the opportunities to come. Get up and make them."*

**Did you know?** Walker was also a patron of the arts and an advocate for African American rights.

## 12 DECEMBER

# Chavela Vargas

Pioneering Ranchera Singer

1919-2012, Costa Rica/Mexico

Chavela Vargas was a Costa Rican-born Mexican singer known for her rendition of ranchera music. She broke gender stereotypes by dressing as a man and singing love songs about women, becoming an iconic figure in Latin American music.

*"In my life, there were always too many things."*

**Did you know?** Vargas came out as a lesbian at the age of 81, becoming an icon for the LGBT community in Latin America.

## 13 DECEMBER

# Amanishakheto

Warrior Queen of Nubia

1st Century BCE, Nubia (Present-day Sudan)

Amanishakheto, a powerful queen of Nubia, known for her military prowess and wealth, skillfully led her kingdom in a time of both war and peace. Her reign was marked by an expansion of the Meroitic Kingdom and an increase in its wealth, largely from gold mines. Amanishakheto's legacy is evident in the numerous temples and pyramids she built, which still stand as testament to her rule.

*"Strength is found not in conquest but in the defense of what is right."*

**Did you know?** Amanishakheto's jewelry, showcased in her tomb, revealed her kingdom's wealth and craftsmanship.

## 14 DECEMBER
# Anne Sullivan
The Miracle Worker

1866-1936, USA

Anne Sullivan, known as the teacher and lifelong companion of Helen Keller, was a remarkable educator. Despite her visual impairments, Sullivan showed an incredible dedication to teaching Keller, who was deaf and blind, to communicate with the world. Her innovative methods revolutionized education for the visually impaired.

*"Keep on beginning and failing. Each time you fail, start all over again, and you will grow stronger until you have accomplished a purpose."*

**Did you know?** Sullivan's teaching approach with Keller was later dubbed "The Sullivan Method."

## 15 DECEMBER

# Beatrix Potter
Beloved Children's Author and Illustrator

1866-1943, United Kingdom

Beatrix Potter was an English writer, illustrator, natural scientist, and conservationist, best known for her children's books featuring animals, such as "The Tale of Peter Rabbit." Potter was a trailblazer in self-publishing her work and left a legacy as a successful woman in the literary world.

*"There is something delicious about writing the first words of a story. You never quite know where they'll take you."*

**Did you know?** Potter was also a respected mycologist, the scientific study of fungi, making significant contributions to the field of botany.

## 16 DECEMBER
# Ethel L. Payne
Pioneering African American Journalist

1911-1991, USA

Ethel L. Payne, known as the "First Lady of the Black Press," was an African American journalist, civil rights activist, and commentator. She was one of the first African American women to achieve national recognition for her coverage of the civil rights movement and international news.

*"The goings-on in America, the racial tensions, had become news all over the world."*

**Did you know?** Payne was the first African American woman to be a radio and television commentator on a national network.

## 17 DECEMBER

# Margaret Chase Smith
Trailblazing American Politician

1897-1995, USA

Margaret Chase Smith was an American politician who served as a U.S. Representative and Senator from Maine. She was the first woman to serve in both houses of Congress and was known for her independent stance and her speech, "Declaration of Conscience," against the tactics of McCarthyism.

*"The right way is not always the popular and easy way. Standing for right when it is unpopular is a true test of moral character."*

**Did you know?** Smith was the first woman to have her name placed in nomination for the presidency at a major party's convention.

## 18 DECEMBER

# Diana Vreeland

Revolutionary Fashion Editor

1903-1989, France/USA

Diana Vreeland was a prominent fashion editor known for her work at Harper's Bazaar and Vogue, and as a special consultant at the Costume Institute of the Metropolitan Museum of Art. Her bold style and vision revolutionized fashion photography and publishing.

*"The eye has to travel."*

**Did you know?** Vreeland's column, "Why Don't You?", in Harper's Bazaar, was famous for its unconventional fashion advice.

## 19 DECEMBER

# Annie Smith Peck
Trailblazing Mountaineer and Suffragist

1850-1935, USA

Annie Smith Peck was an American mountaineer and suffragist. She became famous for her climbing feats, including summiting Mount Huascarán in Peru. Peck was a staunch advocate for women's rights, often climbing in trousers instead of skirts to challenge gender norms of her era.

*"Climbing is as close as we can come to flying."*

**Did you know?** Peck once planted a "Votes for Women" banner on a summit she climbed.

## 20 DECEMBER

# Clara Lemlich

Labor Activist and Leader of the
Uprising of the 20,000

1886-1982, Ukraine/USA

Clara Lemlich was a labor activist and leader of the Uprising of the 20,000, the massive strike of garment workers in New York City in 1909. Her fiery speech ignited the walkout, marking a significant moment in labor history, particularly for women workers' rights.

*"I am one of those who suffers from the abuses described here, and I move that we go on a general strike."*

**Did you know?** Lemlich continued to be active in labor and community organizing throughout her life.

## 21 DECEMBER

# Lise Meitner

Pioneering Nuclear Physicist

1878-1968, Austria/Sweden

Lise Meitner was an Austrian-Swedish physicist who worked on radioactivity and nuclear physics. Meitner was part of the team that discovered nuclear fission, a breakthrough that led to the development of nuclear energy and weapons, but she was overlooked for the Nobel Prize.

*"Science makes people reach selflessly for truth and objectivity; it teaches people to accept reality, with wonder and admiration."*

**Did you know?** Element 109, Meitnerium, is named in her honor.

## 22 DECEMBER
# Clara Zetkin
Women's Rights Advocate and Marxist Theorist

1857-1933, Germany

Clara Zetkin was a German Marxist theorist, activist, and advocate for women's rights. She played a significant role in the international socialist movement and was a driving force behind the establishment of International Women's Day.

> *"I am convinced that the emancipation of women and their equality with men are necessary for the liberation of the human race."*

**Did you know?** Zetkin's efforts led to the first International Women's Day being celebrated in 1911.

## 23 DECEMBER

# George Sand

Pioneering French Novelist and Memoirist

1804-1876, France

George Sand, born Amantine Lucile Aurore Dupin, was one of the most successful female writers of the 19th century. Known for her novels and memoirs, Sand broke gender norms by adopting a male pseudonym and wearing men's clothing, which gave her access to literary and artistic circles otherwise reserved for men. Her works explored themes of love, gender, and society, and she was an advocate for women's rights and social reform.

> *"The beauty of a woman is not in the clothes she wears, the figure that she carries, or the way she combs her hair."*

**Did you know?** Sand had famous relationships with several prominent artists and writers, including Frédéric Chopin.

## 24 DECEMBER

# Jovita Idar

Journalist and Civil Rights Activist

1885-1946, USA

Jovita Idar was a Mexican-American journalist, activist, and suffragist, known for her work in supporting the civil rights of Mexican Americans and women. She wrote for and ran her family's newspaper, La Crónica, which focused on issues such as segregation, racial injustice, and women's rights. Idar was also a founding member of the League of Mexican Women.

*"We have to fight against ignorance and iniquity."*

**Did you know?** Idar is known for standing up to Texas Rangers who wanted to shut down her newspaper for its advocacy.

## 25 DECEMBER

# Benazir Bhutto

First Woman Prime Minister of a
Muslim-majority Country

1953-2007, Pakistan

Benazir Bhutto was a Pakistani politician who served as Prime Minister of Pakistan, becoming the first woman to head a Muslim-majority country. Bhutto, known for her charismatic authority and political astuteness, played a significant role in moving Pakistan towards civilian rule and sought to implement social reforms.

> *"Democracy is necessary to peace and to undermining the forces of terrorism."*

**Did you know?** Bhutto's government was the first in the world to elect a woman to head a Muslim-majority country.

## 26 DECEMBER
# Diana, Princess of Wales
Humanitarian and Cultural Icon

1961-1997, United Kingdom

Diana, Princess of Wales, was a member of the British royal family and a global icon known for her humanitarian and charity work. She was renowned for her compassion and commitment to numerous causes, including the campaign against landmines and supporting people affected by HIV/AIDS.

*"Everyone needs to be valued. Everyone has the potential to give something back."*

**Did you know?** Diana's elegance and style made her an icon in the fashion world.

## 27 DECEMBER

# Sarah E. Goode

Inventor and Entrepreneur

c. 1855-1905, USA

Sarah E. Goode was the first African American woman to receive a United States patent, inventing a folding cabinet bed which helped people maximize their limited space. Her invention paved the way for future innovations in space-saving furniture. Goode's work as an entrepreneur and inventor broke barriers for African American women in business and innovation.

*"Innovation isn't just about the big breakthroughs. It's also about the small steps taken every day."*

**Did you know?** Goode's invention was a precursor to the modern fold-down Murphy bed.

## 28 DECEMBER

# Marjane Satrapi
Graphic Novelist and Filmmaker

1969-Present, Iran/France

Marjane Satrapi is an Iranian-born French graphic novelist, cartoonist, illustrator, and film director. She is best known for her autobiographical graphic novel "Persepolis," which recounts her experiences before and after the Islamic Revolution in Iran. Her work is acclaimed for its unique blend of humor, memoir, and commentary on social issues.

*"Life is too short to be lived badly."*

**Did you know?** "Persepolis" was adapted into an Academy Award-nominated animated film.

## 29 DECEMBER

# Tammy Duckworth

U.S. Senator and Veteran

1968-Present, USA

Tammy Duckworth is an American politician and retired Army National Guard lieutenant colonel serving as the junior United States Senator from Illinois. A U.S. Army veteran, Duckworth lost both of her legs and damaged her right arm when her helicopter was shot down in Iraq, earning her a Purple Heart. She is the first Thai-American woman elected to Congress, the first person born in Thailand elected to Congress, the first woman with a disability elected to Congress, and the first female double amputee in the Senate.

> *"America's veterans embody the ideals upon which America was founded more than 229 years ago."*

**Did you know?** Duckworth played a crucial role in advocating for veterans' rights and benefits.

## 30 DECEMBER

# Empress Matilda
Lady of the English

1102-1167, England

Empress Matilda, also known as Maude, was one of the claimants to the English throne during the civil war known as the Anarchy. A powerful woman of her time, she fought for her right to rule in a male-dominated society. Her conflict with Stephen of Blois for the throne marked a significant period in English history.

*"I am a woman, but I would rather be a queen."*

**Did you know?** Matilda's eventual agreement with Stephen led to her son becoming King Henry II.

## 31 DECEMBER

# Jacqueline Cochran
Record-Breaking Aviator

1906-1980, USA

Jacqueline Cochran was an American pilot and the first woman to break the sound barrier. She was an important contributor to the formation of the Women's Auxiliary Army Corps (WAAC) and Women Airforce Service Pilots (WASP) during World War II. Cochran holds more speed, distance, and altitude records than any other pilot, male or female.

> *"I might have been born in a hovel, but I am determined to travel with the wind and the stars."*

**Did you know?** Cochran was also the first woman to fly a bomber across the Atlantic.

## 365 INSPIRING WOMEN

# BONUS

# Katherine Johnson

Pioneering Mathematician and Space Scientist

1918-2020, USA

Katherine Johnson was an African American mathematician whose calculations of orbital mechanics were critical to the success of the first U.S. crewed spaceflights. Working at NASA, she played a vital role in the early years of the U.S. space program. Her work included calculating trajectories for the Space Shuttle program and the Apollo moon landing mission.

*"I loved going to work every single day."*

**Did you know?** Johnson's story was highlighted in the 2016 film "Hidden Figures."

# Boudica

Warrior Queen of the Iceni

1st Century CE, Ancient Britain

Boudica was a queen of the British Celtic Iceni tribe who led an uprising against the occupying forces of the Roman Empire. Her courage and determination made her a symbol of the struggle for justice and independence, and her legend has endured through the centuries.

*"We British are used to women commanders in war."*

**Did you know?** Boudica's army succeeded in defeating a Roman legion and destroying several major Roman settlements before she was ultimately defeated.

# Queen Bilquis
## The Queen of Sheba

10th Century BCE, Saba (Present-day Yemen/Ethiopia)

Queen Bilquis, also known as the Queen of Sheba, is a figure first mentioned in the Hebrew Bible. She is famed for her visit to King Solomon in Jerusalem, bringing gifts and testing his wisdom with riddles. Bilquis is celebrated for her wisdom, wealth, and ruling capabilities.

*"The wisdom of the land is not measured by its riches but by the hearts and minds of its people."*

**Did you know?** The story of Queen Bilquis is also mentioned in the Quran and other Islamic texts.

## Isadora Duncan
Mother of Modern Dance

1877-1927, USA/Europe

Isadora Duncan was an American dancer who performed to acclaim throughout Europe. Breaking with conventional ballet techniques, Duncan founded a new approach to dance that emphasized natural movement. She is considered one of the founders of modern dance.

*"The dancer's body is simply the luminous manifestation of the soul."*

**Did you know?** Duncan's dance style was influenced by Greek arts, folk dances, social dances, and nature.

# Margaret Mead

Renowned Cultural Anthropologist

1901-1978, USA

Margaret Mead was an American cultural anthropologist who was a prominent author and speaker in the 1960s and 1970s. She earned her fame with her studies and publications on cultural anthropology and her insights into the societal impacts of adolescence and child-rearing in different cultures.

*"Always remember that you are absolutely unique. Just like everyone else."*

**Did you know?** Mead's work in Samoa challenged Western perceptions of gender roles and sexuality.

# Mary Kay Ash

Entrepreneur and Founder of Mary Kay Cosmetics

1918-2001, USA

Mary Kay Ash was an American businesswoman and founder of Mary Kay Cosmetics, Inc. She started her company in a male-dominated industry with a $5,000 investment, growing it into a billion-dollar business. Ash is known for empowering women by providing them with entrepreneurial opportunities.

*"Don't limit yourself. Many people limit themselves to what they think they can do."*

**Did you know?** Mary Kay Ash wrote three best-selling books on business and leadership.

# Zaha Hadid

Visionary Architect

1950-2016, Iraq/United Kingdom

Zaha Hadid was an Iraqi-British architect known for her radical deconstructivist designs. As the first woman to receive the Pritzker Architecture Prize, she broke gender barriers in architecture. Her notable works include the London Aquatics Centre for the 2012 Olympics and the Heydar Aliyev Center in Baku.

*"I really believe in the idea of the future."*

**Did you know?** Hadid's designs were often considered futuristic and unconventional.

# Sappho

Ancient Greek Poet

c. 630-570 BCE, Greece

Sappho was an ancient Greek poet from the island of Lesbos, renowned for her lyric poetry, often focusing on themes of love and passion. Only fragments of her work survive, but her influence on the lyrical poetry genre is undeniable.

*"Someone, I tell you, in another time, will remember us."*

**Did you know?** The terms "sapphic" and "lesbian" derive from Sappho and her association with Lesbos.

# Ana de Sousa Nzingha Mbande

Fearless Queen of Ndongo and Matamba

1583-1663, Angola

Ana de Sousa Nzingha Mbande, known as Queen Nzinga, was a 17th-century queen of the Ndongo and Matamba Kingdoms of the Mbundu people in Angola. She was a resilient leader who fought against the Portuguese and their expanding slave trade in Central Africa. Nzinga was known for her brilliant diplomatic tactics and military strategies, which she used to foster alliances and protect her people.

*"I am a woman, but I am also a king."*

**Did you know?** Queen Nzinga was fluent in Portuguese and was a skillful negotiator, often directly engaging with the Portuguese colonial authorities.

# Gabriela Silang

Revolutionary Leader in the Philippines

1731-1763, Philippines

Gabriela Silang was a Filipina revolutionary leader best known as the first female leader of a Filipino movement for independence from Spain. After her husband's assassination, who was leading the revolt, Silang took over the command and led her people with immense courage against the Spanish forces.

*"I will not let my people down; I will fight until my last breath."*

**Did you know?** Silang is remembered as a national heroine in the Philippines, and numerous schools, roads, and public buildings are named after her.

# Dihya

Warrior Queen of the Berber People

7th Century, North Africa

Dihya, also known as Kahina, was a Berber warrior queen and religious and military leader who led indigenous resistance to the Arab expansion in Northwest Africa. A symbol of resistance in Algeria and Tunisia, she was known for her military skills and strategic acumen in combat.

*"I fight as a free woman, defending my people and my land."*

**Did you know?** Dihya is still celebrated in the Maghreb as a powerful symbol of resistance against foreign invasion.

# Emily Carr
Canadian Artist and Writer

1871-1945, Canada

Emily Carr was a Canadian artist and writer inspired by the Indigenous peoples of the Pacific Northwest Coast. One of the first artists to attempt capturing the spirit of Canada in a modern style, Carr's work was not widely recognized until later in her life.

*"Art is art, nature is nature, you cannot improve upon it."*

**Did you know?** Carr also wrote several autobiographical books about her life, which are now Canadian classics.

# Maria Sibylla Merian

Naturalist and Scientific Illustrator

1647-1717, Germany

Maria Sibylla Merian was a German-born naturalist and scientific illustrator. She is considered among the first entomologists, particularly in her detailed observations and documentation of the metamorphosis of the butterfly. Her artistic work, especially in her book "Metamorphosis Insectorum Surinamensium," is considered highly influential in botany and zoology.

*"Through my work, I hope to arouse the love of nature and art."*

**Did you know?** Merian's work was groundbreaking in changing misconceptions about insects and their life cycles.

## Shirin Ebadi

Nobel Peace Prize Laureate and
Human Rights Activist

1947-Present, Iran

Shirin Ebadi is an Iranian lawyer, former judge, and human rights activist. In 2003, she was awarded the Nobel Peace Prize for her efforts to promote human rights, especially those of women, children, and political prisoners in Iran. She was the first Iranian and the first Muslim woman to receive the prize.

*"I maintain that nothing useful and lasting can emerge from violence."*

**Did you know?** Ebadi founded the Defenders of Human Rights Center in Iran.

# Ellen Johnson Sirleaf

First Elected Female Head of State in Africa

1938-Present, Liberia

Ellen Johnson Sirleaf is a Liberian politician who served as the 24th President of Liberia. She was the first elected female head of state in Africa and was awarded the 2011 Nobel Peace Prize for her efforts to further women's rights and peaceful reconciliation following Liberia's long civil war.

*"If your dreams do not scare you, they are not big enough."*

**Did you know?** Sirleaf's government focused on promoting peace and rebuilding Liberia's economy and infrastructure.

## Louise Bourgeois
Influential French-American Artist and Sculptor

1911-2010, France/USA

Louise Bourgeois was a renowned French-American artist and sculptor, best known for her large-scale sculpture and installation art. Her work, often themed on exploring family, sexuality, and the body, was groundbreaking in its openness and depth. Bourgeois' famous piece, "Maman," a giant spider sculpture, symbolizes strength and fragility.

*"Art is a guarantee of sanity."*

**Did you know?** Bourgeois used art to work through her experiences and emotions, often drawing from her tumultuous childhood.

Printed in Great Britain
by Amazon